Leslie Orrey
was born at Hawnby in Yorkshire in 1908.
From 1945 to 1969 he was Lecturer and then Head of the Music Department of Goldsmiths' College, University of London, as well as Visiting Professor at various American universities. He wrote books on harmony, Bellini, Gluck and programme music, and died in 1981. Rodney Milnes is one of Britain's leading opera critics. In 1986 he took over the editorship of *Opera* magazine.

# Opera

## A Concise History

Revised and updated edition by Rodney Milnes

**Leslie Orrey**

253 illustrations, 32 in color

**Thames and Hudson**

*To Elsa*



*This revised and updated edition first published in the United States in 1987 by Thames and Hudson Inc., 500 Fifth Avenue, New York, New York 10110*

*Library of Congress Catalog Card Number 86-51512*

*Previously published in the USA as* A Concise History of Opera



*Printed and bound in Singapore by Che San*

## Contents

## Preface

A good, succinct definition of opera is hard to come by. The word 'opera' itself is far from satisfactory, in that it harbours too many built-in prejudices and begs too many questions; some such term as 'lyric stage' is perhaps to be preferred. The standpoint adopted in this book is that 'opera' is not an isolated form but a branch of the theatre, and deserves to be considered as such. Its essentials are dramatic confrontation and dialogue, intensified by music both on stage and in the orchestra. Like true drama, it transcends mere narrative.

Its sub-categories also resist simple definition: *opéra-comique* is not necessarily 'comic' opera; *opera seria* is 'serious' opera in only one rather narrow aspect; 'operetta' has come to mean something more specific than merely 'a little opera'; and so on. Moreover, the categories overlap to such an extent that attempts at strict definition can become confusing. I have tried to give sufficient detail for the broad divisions to be clear.

The criss-cross of styles, movements and languages precludes a straightforward narrative on simple chronological lines, and, whatever arrangement is adopted, some backtracking is unavoidable. For example, in the early seventeenth century opera (defined then as 'dramma per musica' – drama through music) spread rapidly from Italy to France and thence to England in a clear, linear sequence. But complications soon set in, and I have preferred to trace the lines of development in the latter two countries right through to the end of the eighteenth century (Chapters Three and Four) before turning to the great Italian operatic colonization of Europe which also began in the seventeenth century, but whose finest flowering was in the eighteenth. Similar problems arose over the nineteenth-century nationalist movements (Chapter Eleven), where the most important, that of Russia, is followed through into the twentieth century to about the 1917 Revolution.

All writers on opera face a language problem. The general principle which I have adopted with regard to titles in French, Italian or German is to give the opera its correct title the first time it is mentioned and thereafter, in so far as is possible, to use its English equivalent. Only important titles, including those of operas in the current repertory, are translated in the body of the text, but all, where translatable, are given in both the original language and in English in the Index. The titles of operas in other languages (for example, Russian or Czech) are given only in English. The Index also gives the years of birth and death of each composer mentioned in the text.

## Preface to revised edition

Preparation of this new edition of the late Leslie Orrey's admirable historical survey has involved substantial alteration only to the last two chapters, which have been brought up to date. Any views expressed about operas premiered since 1972 or recent trends in production are thus mine. Otherwise Mr Orrey's text stands, save for the correction of one or two slips and some minor adjustments made in the light of such unforeseen events as the recent revival of interest in Rossini's serious operas and the ever more frequent performance (and recording) of Baroque and pre-Classical works. A handful of up-to-date illustrations have been included, and I have added some recently published books to the bibliography.

Rodney Milnes, *August 1986*

1, 2, 3 *Right:* The plan of the SS. Giovanni e Paolo theatre, opened in Venice in 1639, shows the familiar U-shape of the auditorium. Francesco Milizia, writing in 1794, conceived his ideal theatre in terms of a semicircular auditorium on the ancient Greek model, and saw it as part of an arts centre complex (*opposite, left*). The 1927 design (*opposite, right*) by Walter Gropius (1883–1969) shows a characteristically stylized conception based on interlocking circles and ellipses.

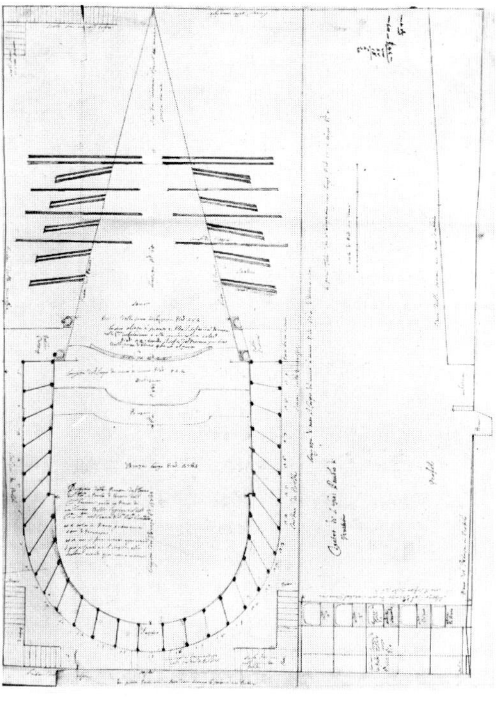

# The Beginnings of Opera in Italy

It is tempting to regard 6 March 1637 as the birth date of opera. On that day, in the parish of San Cassiano in Venice, the first commercial opera house opened its doors, to a public that paid for admission, and on whose support the venture relied for its success.

A second public opera house, opened two years later, is known in some detail since a plan is preserved in the Sir John Soane Museum in London. From this, and from descriptions by contemporaries who visited Italy during the seventeenth century, we can piece together a fairly reliable picture of the sophisticated entertainment we call opera as it was then, and which would differ little in essentials from nineteenth- or twentieth-century experience.

John Evelyn went to the opera in Venice in 1645, and wrote thus in his *Diary*: 'This night, having with my Lord Bruce taken our places before, we went to the Opera, where comedies and other plays are

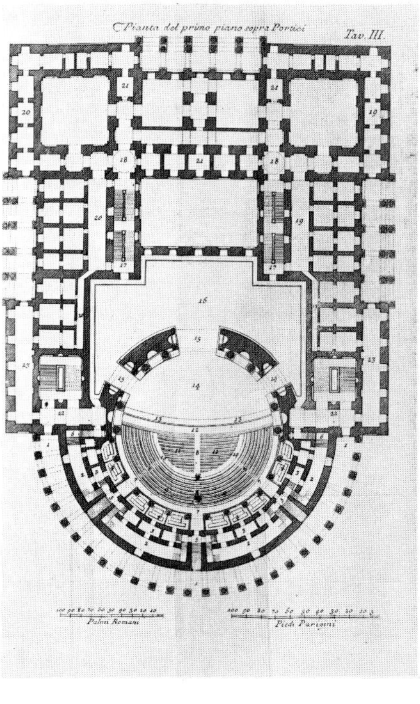


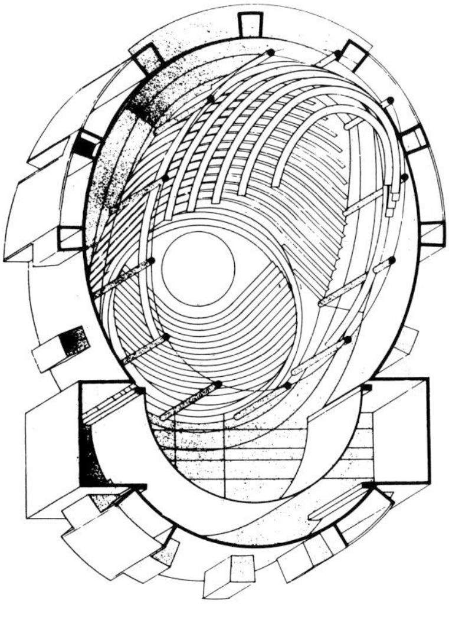

4 Fragment from a French manuscript from Saint-Benoît-sur-Loire; a portion of a liturgical drama.

represented in recitative music, by the most excellent musicians, vocal and instrumental, with variety of scenes painted and contrived with no less art of perspective, and machines for flying in the air, and other wonderful notions; taken together, it is one of the most magnificent and expensive diversions the wit of man can invent.'

But the date 1637 is deceptively convenient, and ignores centuries of fascinating developments as well as implying too narrow a definition of opera. Just as for the ancient Greeks drama was primarily a religious experience, so the medieval church, seeking every means to promote the Christian message, was quick to realize drama's power in bringing home the essentials of this message to a largely illiterate congregation. Such 'liturgical' plays are known from at least as early as the tenth century, and a fair number survive. One French 4
manuscript, originating at Saint-Benoît-sur-Loire and now in the Orleans library, contains no fewer than ten such plays, with music; and the indications given here and in other sources as to costumes, action and scenery leave no doubt that we are dealing with works that contain all the ingredients of opera. The Easter Visitation to the Sepulchre and the Christmas story were popular subjects, and a few

5 Goliath slain by David. This 'narrative' picture from Bergamo, showing at least three simultaneous 'scenes', gives some indication of the next development, when the play was presented outside the church.

6 This somewhat crude drawing, from a Ms in the Bodleian Library, Oxford, perhaps represents a puppet show, but it might equally show part of a pageant.

plays were drawn from the Old Testament: one of these, *The Play of Daniel*, has been published in modern editions, and in performance has revealed itself as remarkably fresh, sincere and moving. The basic ingredients were the liturgical text, in Latin, to which supplementary verses in the vernacular were added; there were solos and choruses, and even some provision for instrumental colour.

These works developed into the somewhat more elaborate Mystery Plays, whose heyday was the thirteenth and fourteenth centuries, and even later. They were widely distributed throughout Europe; those in Italy, known as *Sacre Rappresentazioni*, are specially pertinent since they lead directly to oratorio and opera. They, too, began in church, but certainly by the fifteenth century had been transferred to other
5 locations, such as the piazza in front of the church. They were for one or more voices, sung throughout, in recitative or in a more formal style. The language was Italian, not Latin, and they were true drama in that the action was propelled by confrontation and dialogue, aided by costumes and scenery. Their exact place in the development of opera is hard to assess since the music has not come down to us, but we do know that besides the liturgical plainsong there were other elements, such as instrumental effects and 'Laudi', or spiritual songs (hymns), sung in the vernacular in a simple, popular idiom.

As the *Sacre Rappresentazioni* moved away from the church
6 precincts they received some cross-fertilization from secular pageants

7 Vittorino da Feltre; a commemorative portrait medal by Antonio Pisanello (*c.* 1395–*c.* 1455).

and entertainments, and this element also leads to the operatic developments of the late sixteenth century.

It was the city-states of northern Italy that played the most vigorous part in this essentially Renaissance movement, with among others the Gonzaga family as benevolent and enlightened patrons. A crucial date is 1425, when Gian Francesco Gonzaga invited Vittorino da Feltre to 7
his court and so established Mantua as a centre of learning and the arts. The work was continued by Gian Francesco's son, Lodovico, who brought the painter Mantegna to Mantua. The musicians connected with the Mantuan court during his reign included Tromboncino, the composer of *frottole* or part-songs which were the ancestors of the madrigal; and, among madrigalists, the Fleming Giaches de Wert. Madrigals play a small part in the story, in that a few madrigal cycles exist which show a coherent narrative form. The best known of these is a set by Orazio Vecchi entitled *L'Amfiparnasso* which, though never intended to be acted, was certainly a step towards opera by reason of its delineation of character in the little vignettes that make up the cycle.

A good deal more significance attaches to the *Orfeo* of Poliziano, a verse drama performed at Mantua probably in 1472. The poem, pastoral in style, is extant, but not the music that went with it, though we know something about it; there was a chorus, there was some ballet, and the instructions printed with the poem make it clear that at least part of it was sung. Another interesting forerunner, also at

8, 9 An engraving by Jacques Callot (1592/3–1635), showing a performance of the ballet, *La liberazione di Tireno*, staged in the Uffizi Palace, Florence, in 1616. In early ballets and masques the 'spectacle' was by no means confined to the area beyond the proscenium arch (see *Ill.* 24), but, as this picture illustrates, could invade the whole theatre. *Ill.* 9 (*right*) depicts another, earlier, lavish entertainment, also in Florence, on the occasion of the wedding of Cosimo de' Medici II and Maria Maddalena of Austria. The scenery and machines were by Giulio Parigi (d. 1635). The scene is the fourth *intermedio* in The Judgment of Paris (1608).

Mantua, was the *Rappresentazione di Dafne* (1486), with music (lost) by Giampietro della Viola. Thereafter there are increasingly frequent records of performances of such dramas, their sumptuousness varying with the occasion, not only in Mantua and Ferrara, but in Florence, Milan, Venice, Rome and Naples, as the great houses of the Sforzas, Viscontis, Gonzagas, d'Estes and Medicis intermarried. Music is frequently mentioned, but is rarely regarded as the most important factor. Occasionally the composer is named, as for example in the production of Giovanni Battista Cinzio's *Orbecche* in 1541 at Ferrara, music (lost) by Alfonso della Viola, scenery and designs by Girolamo Carpi of Ferrara. Carpi was not the only painter, or indeed the most famous, to be called in for these spectacles: in 1483, in Milan, for the wedding of Gian Galeazzo Sforza to Isabella d'Aragon, the decorations had been devised by Leonardo da Vinci, and in Rome, in 1519, there had been a performance of Lodovico Ariosto's pastoral drama *I Suppositi*, with scenery by Raphael.

9 Often it was the interludes (*intermedi*) between the acts of the play

itself that formed the truest links with opera. The wedding festivities in Florence in 1539 at the marriage of Duke Cosimo I de' Medici and Eleonora of Toledo included a comedy, *Il Comodo*, by Antonio Landi; the *intermedi* contained madrigals by Francesco Corteccia, who also contributed music for some of the *intermedi* (based on the legend of Cupid and Psyche) at another Medici wedding in 1565 in Florence, and it is clear from contemporary descriptions that there was not only instrumental accompaniment to the singing but also an instrumental *entr'acte* calling for a sizable orchestra – four harpsichords, four viols, two sackbuts (trombones), two lutes, two tenor recorders, a flute and a cornett.

The most celebrated and perhaps the most lavish of these entertainments was that of 1589 at the wedding of Ferdinando de' Medici with Christine of Lorraine, in Florence. The moving spirit was the architect Bernardo Buontalenti. There were six *intermedi* inserted in a play, *La Pellegrina* ('The Pilgrim'); one of these, *Il Combattimento pitici d'Apollo col Serpente* ('Apollo's Victory over the Python'), was later amplified by the poet Ottavio Rinuccini into what may with justice be claimed as the first opera, *Dafne*, the first recorded performance of which was at Florence in 1598. All but two fragments of the music, by Jacopo Peri, are lost, but contemporary testimonies to its excellence include that of the composer Marco da Gagliano, who set the same text in 1608 and in his preface remarked of Peri's music, 'The pleasure and the amazement of those present was beyond expression.' The subject was a popular one; the same libretto formed the basis a few years later of the first German opera, by Heinrich Schütz, given at Torgau, near Dresden (music lost).

Another popular story was that of Orpheus and Eurydice. Poliziano's *Orfeo* had been frequently repeated, and the subject had also appeared from time to time as an *intermedio*, for example in a play, *Armenia*, by G.B. Visconti, in 1599. But its first appearance in something like the form we would recognize as an opera was in 1600, when, as part of the Florentine festivities during the wedding of Maria de' Medici with Henri IV of France, the following were given: *La contesa fra Giunone e Minerva*, words by G.B. Guarini, music by Emilio de' Cavalieri; *Euridice*, words by Rinuccini, music mainly by Peri (with a few numbers contributed by Giulio Caccini); and a pastoral drama, *Il Rapimento di Cefalo*, words by Gabriello Chiabrera, music by Caccini. Caccini rapidly produced, in addition, a rival version of *Euridice*, which, like Peri's, was in vocal score, with a figured bass. The full orchestral score was not customary until fifty or sixty years later, so that when these old operas are mounted today the precise disposition of the orchestral forces is a combination of guesswork and scholarly intuition, even when the composer has indicated the total orchestral resource at his command.

These theatrical experiments grew out of a conscious attempt to re-create a type of performance about which scarcely any precise details were known. When Italian Renaissance scholars, seeking spiritual regeneration in the golden age of classical Greece, turned their attention to drama they immediately came upon a difficulty. Music, it was clear, played a considerable part; the Greek chorus, for example, acting as a sort of engaged commentator, certainly sang, or chanted, for part of the time. Some of the main characters may also have sung, or declaimed; there was also dancing, and there was some use of instruments such as the *kithara* or the *aulos* (Harrison Birtwistle's music for Peter Hall's production of the *Oresteia* at the National Theatre,

10 Apollo about to descend to attack the 'python'; the third *intermedio*, devised by Bernardo Buontalenti (1536–1608), for the 1589 Florence festivities.

London, 1981, was a convincing modern reconstruction). But in the absence of written evidence we are and will remain in the dark as to what precisely this music was.

Among those who addressed themselves to this problem in Florence during the last decade of the sixteenth century was a group of thinkers who have become known as the Florentine Camerata. They met at the house of a wealthy patron, Count Bardi, and their members included, as well as Rinuccini, Peri and Caccini, the composer Vincenzo Galilei (the father of the astronomer). Between them they evolved the idea of *recitativo* – a single vocal line, sung in a free, declamatory style, with simple instrumental support. This, solely concerned to reflect the meaning of the words and the inner life of the drama, did not impede the poet's thought as did the contrapuntal madrigal style. It was even argued that it was superior to spoken verse, since the musical inflections intensified the implied emotions.

Caccini's publication, *Le Nuove Musiche* ('The New Music', 1602), outlined the theory and gave practical examples, while the *Euridice* mentioned above showed its application to the drama.

But Peri and Caccini were no more than competent practitioners, and something else was needed if these ventures were to be raised beyond the level of interesting experiments. The man who elevated
11 the New Music to the realm of high art was Claudio Monteverdi (1567–1643), one of the great musical geniuses of all time.

11 Claudio Monteverdi (1567–1643), born at Cremona in northern Italy, was 1602–12 in the employ of the duke of Mantua, during which time *Orfeo* and *Arianna* were written. From 1613 he lived in Venice, where his last two operas were written for the public theatres.

## Monteverdi. Opera in Seventeenth-century Rome and Venice

By the time Monteverdi was invited to present a *favola in musica* for the pleasure of the Accademia degl'Invaghiti in Mantua in 1607, the Italians had a wide range of experience to draw upon, and there was little that was beyond them in stage presentation. The principle of movable scenery was understood, and heavenly apparitions and cloud transformations, developed from Brunelleschi (the *paradiso* in the church of San Felice in Florence attributed to him is described in vivid detail in Vasari's *Lives of the Artists*), were common. Alessandro Striggio, the poet of the new opera, was Chancellor to the Mantuan court; he had a musical background (his father was a composer of madrigals), and was in close contact with the Camerata. Above all, Monteverdi, now thirty-nine years old and with an established reputation, was the one man with the musical ability and force of personality to give artistic and dramatic life to the theories of the Camerata.

The time was ripe for a miracle – a word that is hardly too strong for *Orfeo*. The entire future of opera lay cradled here, already developed 13
far beyond the embryonic stage. Monteverdi, who had thoroughly assimilated the new monodic style, was equally well versed in the older techniques, and the madrigal, which in *L'Amfiparnasso* had not quite won its dramatic spurs, in *Orfeo* slips into place quite naturally, underlining the pastoral quality of the play on the one hand, while on the other etching in with superb effect the terrible pathos of the blow dealt Orfeo by the news of Euridice's death. The balletic quality of the music is striking, the instrumental versatility no less so. Monteverdi was as aware as Verdi or Wagner of the potency of instrumental timbre, and the large assortment of instruments he demanded was a pool from which he could draw the appropriate tone colours as required. Above all he had the power to draft his music on a large scale; the unity is a musical unity, the sections repeating and balancing with the sureness of a Beethoven symphony.

12 Adriana Basile (*c.* 1580–*c.* 1640), contralto, the first of the 'star' singers, with a great reputation all over Italy. Monteverdi thought very highly of her, and may well have conceived the part of Orfeo with her in mind, though it is not known if she ever sang it.

13 (*right*) The opening of the first act of *Orfeo*, reproduced from a contemporary edition. The 1607 performance, not being the occasion of a princely wedding, was not written about with the fullness and wealth of detail of some earlier performances (for example, the 1589 festivities mentioned on *page* 16). The score was first published in 1609 by the Venetian firm of Amadino.

In the following year the most important social event was the wedding of Francesco Gonzaga to Margherita of Savoy, and this prompted a feast of theatrical entertainment almost as lavish as the 1589 wedding of Ferdinando de' Medici. Monteverdi's opera *Arianna* was produced, while Marco da Gagliano's *Dafne* was given earlier in the year, during the pre-wedding carnival celebrations. The superb 'lament' from the former, which is all of it that is preserved, was to be the prototype of many, including that of Dido in Purcell's *Dido and Aeneas*.

The new kind of entertainment spread rapidly to neighbouring cities in Tuscany and Lombardy, as well as further south to Rome and Naples, and beyond the shores of Italy. It chiefly took the form of dramas or pastorals drawn either from classical mythology or from earlier Italian sources, for example Giovanni Battista Guarini's *Il Pastor fido* or Torquato Tasso's *Gerusalemme liberata*; but Rome was already providing some interesting variants. Its somewhat chequered early operatic history is linked not only with wealthy church dignitaries such as Cardinal Barberini, who had an imposing opera

RITORNELLO

# PROLOGO

## LA MVSICA.

Al mio permeſſo a mato a uoi ne uegno Incliti Eroi
ſangue gentil de Regi Di cui narra la famma ec celſi pregi Ne giũge al uer perch'è trop
p'alto il ſegno
Ritornello

house built in his palace in 1623, but with a pious and zealous priest, Philip Neri, who, in the chapel or 'oratory' which he built, harnessed music to a popular, 'revivalist' type of service. It was here, in 1600, that a sacred drama, *La Rappresentatione di Anima, et di Corpo* ('The Drama of the Soul and the Body'), was first performed This, usually spoken of as the first 'oratorio' (the name is derived from the place where it was performed), is another link between church and theatre, for it is to be noted that it was acted, with scenery and costumes. The composer was Cavalieri, who had already written three musical pastorals (now lost); like the earlier liturgical dramas, it was in the new 'recitative' style, and in dialogue form; like them, too, it used abstractions, 'the Soul', 'the Body', and so on, for its *dramatis personae*. It has had a long line of hybrid successors, half oratorio, half opera, some of which will be noted in later chapters.

The first opera to be performed in Cardinal Barberini's opera house also shows some notable deviations in form and content from
14 Mantuan and Florentine opera. *San Alessio*, with a libretto by another churchman, Cardinal Rospigliosi, and music by Stefano Landi, instead of relying on classical mythology deals with the legend of the fifth-century saint Alexis. Landi's music is interesting in many respects, for instance the orchestra takes a distinct step towards the modern conception, the more assertive violins pushing the gentler viols on one side, and the treatment generally leaning towards the tightly organized string orchestra of Lully a few years later. Another feature was the inclusion of comic scenes. Comedy had played no part in the first operas, and was later to be banished again from the *opera seria* (see Chapter Five), but it found a welcome in Venetian opera, while in Rome Rospigliosi was the author of two works that are truly comic operas. They were *Chi soffre speri* ('Who suffers, may hope'), with music by Virgilio Mazzocchi and Marco Marazzoli, produced in the Barberini theatre, 1637; and *Dal male il bene* ('From Evil comes Good'), produced in 1653 – a work that already displays the comic servant and other characteristics that were to become the staple ingredients of eighteenth-century comic opera.

A city that, in slightly different circumstances, might have played a crucial part in the early days of opera was Parma. The reigning Duke of Parma, Ranucci Farnese I, had been fêted on a royal scale in Florence in 1604, when among other entertainments Peri's *Dafne* was repeated. It was some years before an opportunity for the fitting

14 A scene from *San Alessio* (Rome, 1634); a typical 'architectural' set, in central perspective, which, like the permanent scenery in the Teatro Olimpico, Vicenza, could do duty for almost any situation.

repayment of this hospitality arose, with a proposed visit to Parma in 1618 of Cosimo II de' Medici, Grand Duke of Tuscany. For this event, which as it happened never took place, a complete theatre was built inside one of the rooms of Ranucci's palace. Constructed of wood, and reputed to accommodate four thousand people, it was well equipped, and was the first large theatre with movable, sliding scenery.

Ranucci did not live to see the inauguration of his splendid new theatre. He died in 1622, and in 1628 his successor, Odoardo, celebrated his marriage to Cosimo's daughter with customary splendour, but the main item, *Mercurio e Marte*, was less an opera than a pageant, an extravaganza of monumental proportions. The music, by Monteverdi, is lost, but the libretto survives. The emphasis was on spectacle; there was an equestrian ballet, and the entertainment concluded with the flooding of the arena, where sea monsters

15 The theatre in the parish of S. Giovanni Crisostomo, built by Tomaso Bezzi for Carlo and Vincenzo Grimani (1672). In the nineteenth century it was renamed Teatro Malibran; although much altered, it is still used for opera.

disported themselves, while Jove with his attendants descended from aloft to give his blessing on the nuptial pair.

The first true opera performed there was *La finta Pazza* ('Feigned Madness'), by Sacrati, in 1644. The libretto by Giulio Strozzi had already been set by Monteverdi, whose opera was probably never performed. In company with several of Monteverdi's works from this period the music has vanished, and our loss is all the greater in that this was a comedy on which he lavished more than ordinary care and attention.

Fortunately we do possess the scores of Monteverdi's last two operas, written when he was over seventy for the public theatres of Venice. Their subjects were drawn from Greek classics (*Il Ritorno*
16 *d'Ulisse in Patria*, 1641) and ancient Roman history (*L'Incoronazione di Poppea*, 1642). The latter, discussed in Chapter Five, has been acclaimed as his masterpiece, a view which modern audiences all over the world have been able to confirm.

The Venetians' enthusiasm for opera was unbounded. Between 1637 and 1700 at least sixteen theatres were built, the number of operas

16 Ottavia (Trudeliese Schmidt) ordering Ottone (Paul Esswood) to kill Poppea. Zurich Opera House production of Monteverdi's *The Coronation of Poppea*, 1977, by Jean-Pierre Ponnelle, conducted by Nikolaus Harnoncourt.

17 (*below*) Cavalli's *Calisto*, revived at Glyndebourne in 1970. James Bowman as Endymion, Federico Davià as Pan.

18, 19 This scene, by Alfonso Parigi, shows the conventional architectural set, with its central axis (cf. *Ill.* 14), and with two diagonal side avenues. *Ill.* 19 (*right*) shows the same scene, in flames. They are from a Florentine libretto of 1620, *Il Solimano*, and give a good idea of the illusions practised in the contemporary theatre (see also *Ills* 28 and 30).

produced running into hundreds. The situation, with each parish boasting its 'neighbourhood' opera house, is comparable to that of the cinema in its heyday in the 1930s. It is possible to list here only a few of the composers who kept this opera factory going.

Francesco Manelli, the composer of *Andromeda*, which opened the San Cassiano opera house in 1637, was not a Venetian but came from Tivoli; he was soon lured away to Parma. The most influential figure in the mid-century was Pier Francesco Cavalli, a pupil of Monteverdi. In his hands certain of the musical aspects of opera (the aria, the overture) began to take a firmer shape; dramatically he was a worthy
17 pupil of his master. *L'Ormindo* (1644) and *La Calisto* (1651), among many of his other operas, have been successfully revived. Slightly later were Antonio Sartorio, Carlo Pallavicino and Pietro Andrea Ziani; Tommaso Albinoni, Antonio Vivaldi, Carlo Francesco Pollarolo and

4

Antonio Pollarolo take us well into the next century and overlap with Handel's Venetian visit in 1709.

As always, the circumstances surrounding the opera dictated the form it should take. Since the productions were commercial ventures, costs had to be considered. Casts were kept to about six or eight singers, and the chorus was either dispensed with altogether or reduced to a 'walk-on' role as soldiers, attendants, and so on, with little or nothing to sing. The orchestra, now firmly established in its place in front of the stage, became standardized as a small string group, with trumpets and drums added occasionally for martial music, flutes (recorders) brought in for the tenderer passages. The decor remained the prime consideration. Though scaled down considerably from the exuberance of the court entertainments, it still must have been the major item of expense, for the Venetians delighted as much as ever in their cloud machines, magical transformations and ambitious lighting effects. *22, 23*

The technical side of stage mechanics was fully described and illustrated in a book by Nicola Sabbatini published in 1638: *Pratica di fabricar scene, e machine ne' teatri*; this was put into practice in Venice by, *20, 21*

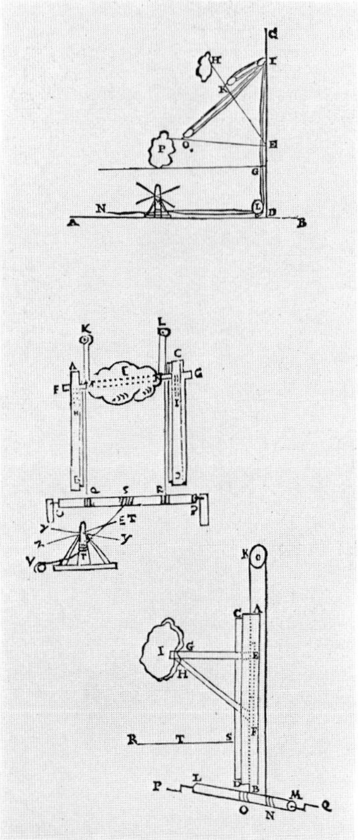

20, 21 Illustrations from Sabbatini's treatise on theatrical machinery, which gives diagrams and detailed instructions for constructing the mechanical devices that made possible such astounding theatrical effects as are shown in *Ills* 21 and 22. *Ill.* 21 (*below*) is from Sacrati's *La Venere gelosa* (Venice, 1643): Apollo's Palace, 'represented and invented' by Giacomo Torelli (1608–78). One 'cloud machine' has descended and disgorged a *corps de ballet*; the upper one contains an orchestra.

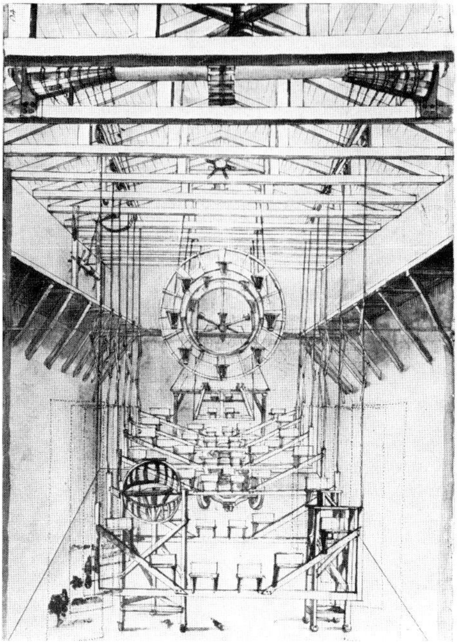

22, 23 A scene from Legrenzi's opera, *Germanico sul Reno* (Venice, 1675). *Ill.* 23 takes us behind the cotton-wool clouds and the painted canvases, and reveals the elaborate system of beams, ropes, wheels, pulleys and platforms which formed the mechanical framework of these stage wonders.

among others, Giacomo Torelli. Torelli was the outstanding stage technician of his day, but was only carrying on the work of Buontalenti. The very first opera publicly performed in Venice, *Andromeda*, was already elaborate, as the account printed in 1637, and quoted in Simon Towneley Worsthorne's *Venetian Opera in the Seventeenth Century*, shows: 'The sky opened and one saw Jove and Juno in glory and other divinities. This great machine descended to the ground to the accompaniment of a concerto of voices and instruments truly from heaven. The two heroes, joined to each other, it conducted to the sky. Here the royal and ever worthy occasion had an end.' The stage spectacle tended to become more lavish and varied as the century wore on.

These sixty years saw crucial developments in the purely musical side of opera. It was a period of intense experimentation in the abstract instrumental forms, and this was bound to affect the opera house. The violin was acquiring its own characteristic idiom (as distinct from the viol), much of which was easily transferable to the voice. The string texture became more flexible and supple; whereas Cavalli in the mid-century on the whole used strings as a monolithic chorus, towards the end of the century the parts became more sinuous and figured, in an interplay of counterpoint presaging Handel and J.S. Bach. In composers such as Vivaldi, Legrenzi and Albinoni, equally skilled in the abstract/instrumental style, there is little to distinguish parts that are sung from those that are played. The vocal line, which in Monteverdi and Cavalli was already edging away from its purist role as drama's handmaid, moved significantly towards the position where its subservience to the needs of dramatic truth was compromised by purely musical considerations: the 'aria' was born. This, formalized, motivic, bound into a coherent musical entity by various 'ostinato' devices (the 'ground bass' was only one of these, though possibly the richest in its potentialities), offered an expressive tool beyond the imagination of the early pioneers. The aria was to dominate opera for a hundred years.

## Opera in France from Lully to the Revolution

In France as in Italy, state occasions such as royal birthdays, weddings and state visits were inseparably associated with pageantry and spectacle. These entertainments mostly concern us only marginally, but one, *Le Balet comique de la Royne*, is of cardinal importance in the 24
history of the theatre, in that spectacle, costume, scenery and music were combined with the dramatic element, in a more or less coherent story that had an exposition, tension and resolution. It was performed on 15 October 1581, at the wedding of the Duke of Joyeuse, a favourite of King Henri III, and Mlle de Vaudemont, the queen's sister; its subject-matter was the Circe legend, and its treatment, a combination of mime, song (solo and chorus) and dancing, was, like the Italian experiments of the time, an attempt to revive ancient Greek practice. Its importance in the history of ballet is paramount, since the Ballet du Cour was derived from it, and thus the way was paved for the evolution of classical ballet; but it also had far-reaching implications for the future of French opera.

The music was composed by two Frenchmen, Lambert de Beaulieu and Jacques Salmon, but the master of ceremonies and guiding spirit was an Italian from Piedmont, Baldassarino de Belgioioso, who had gallicized his name to Balthazar de Beaujoyeulx. The Italian artistic influence had been strong in France ever since François I had begun assembling Italian workmen at Fontainebleau, and was if anything intensified under the influence of two Italian consorts, Catherine de' Medici, wife of Henri II, and Maria de' Medici, wife of Henri IV and mother of Louis XIII, while in the seventeenth century the French theatre was for a time dominated by the personality of the Sicilian Giulio Mazarini (Mazarin). Mazarin arrived in Paris as Papal Legate in 1634, became a Cardinal, and on the death of Richelieu in 1642 took over the duties of Prime Minister and became the most influential figure in France.

Among the Italian musicians who came to Paris under his protection was the composer Luigi Rossi, whose *Orfeo* was presented

24 (*left*) *Le Balet comique de la Royne*, 1581; an engraving by Jacques Patin.

25 Jean-Baptiste Lully was the first operatic composer to achieve international fame. During the seventeenth century his works were played not only in Paris, Versailles and other French cities such as Lyons and Bordeaux, but also in centres such as Hamburg, Munich and Stockholm. He wrote, or collaborated in, more than sixty works for the stage: ballets and comédies-ballets and eighteen operas.

at the Palais Royal in 1647, before the young King Louis XIV, aged nine. Torelli, too, was lured away from Venice, and in 1650 Parisians were able to admire the cunning of his theatrical machines in Corneille's *Andromède*. Ten years later, for the marriage of Louis XIV and Maria Teresa of Spain, Cavalli was invited to Paris to give his *Xerse*, with scenery and machines also by Torelli, and enlivened with ballets by yet another Italian, a young Florentine named Giovanni Battista Lulli (Lully).

Lully (1632–87) exerted an influence on French music in the 25
seventeenth century comparable to that of Handel in eighteenth-century England. French dramatic music was just finding its feet. In 1659 the poet Pierre Perrin collaborated with the composer Robert Cambert to produce an entertainment, *La Pastorale d'Issy*, which, though apparently more idyllic than dramatic (the score has not been preserved) seemed to offer a French challenge to the Italian ideal. It was so successful that both authors received official encouragement from the court, and a few years later, in 1669, the Académie Royale de Musique (the Opéra) was established, Perrin being granted a monopoly of operatic production. In 1671 he and Cambert produced what may well be described as the first French opera, *Pomone*.

Unfortunately neither was strong enough to withstand the more powerful personality of Lully. He had arrived in Paris as a boy of fourteen, in the service of Mlle de Montpensier, and his natural abilities as both dancer and violinist, coupled with superabundant

26 Louis XIV (1638–1715) during his long reign not only took an active part in the planning of court entertainments but participated in them – indoors or out of doors. Extravagance of costume vied with the splendours of the scenery.

energy, driving ambition and (at least so his enemies said) a capacity for intrigue, soon brought him to the notice and favour of the young
26 Louis XIV. Sharing the king's passion for dancing (out of which was created the new art of ballet) and enjoying his protection and confidence, Lully was soon in an unassailable position.

Lully also established contact with one of France's most remarkable men of the theatre, Molière, dancer, actor and playwright, and out of their collaboration arose a new conception, the Comédie-Ballet. This was a highly stylized blend of singing, dancing, comedy and spectacle; in such works as *Le Mariage forcé* (1664), *La Princesse d'Elide* (1664) and, above all, *Le Bourgeois Gentilhomme* (1670), Lully displayed a light and elegant touch which was the counterpart of Molière's wit. The Comédie-Ballet is to some extent the ancestor of the later comedies in music, but its immediate importance was as a link with the next stage of French opera.

Perrin's Académie Royale de Musique was hardly launched before it was in trouble, and in 1672 the king granted a new privilege to Lully which, in effect, ensured him the monopoly of opera in Paris. In the following year Lully brought out *Cadmus et Hermione*, the first of the long series of operas written in collaboration with Philippe Quinault.
27, 31 In this and those that followed (*Alceste*, 1674; *Atys*, 1676; *Proserpine*,
28, 30 1680; *Armide*, 1686), Lully set a pattern for French opera that endured

for almost a hundred years, with little change in essentials, and which was still exerting its influence even in the nineteenth century.

The essence of the Lullian *tragédie en musique* is to be found in the recitative; by modelling his melodic style on the declamation of the best actors, by close attention to the rhythms and cadences of French poetry, then at its most superb and stately (this was the era not only of Corneille, Quinault and Molière, but also of Racine), he set the French language in a simple, accompanied recitative that faithfully mirrored the inflexions while allowing free play to the dramatic or poetic content. The 'air' was the French equivalent of the Italian aria, but lacked the importance and the purely musical organization which the latter was already receiving in Italian hands. It played a subsidiary role, and in fact the air has never dominated French opera in the way the aria has Italian. By contrast, the dance was given an emphasis that has had an abiding influence on the course of French opera. This we owe to the king's passion for the ballet, but Lully, also a dancer, was happy

27 A performance of Lully's *Alceste* in the open air at Versailles (1674), lit by *une infinité de lumières* (some can be clearly seen, all round the base of the Mansard roof, and right on top of the roof at the back). The orchestra, split in two so that the king (centre) might have an uninterrupted view, consists of about forty players.

28 *Armide* (1686) was the last opera in which Lully collaborated with Philippe Quinault (1635–88). The story derives from Tasso's *Gerusalemme liberata*; in the last act Armide resolves to destroy herself, together with the palace and garden which she has magically created, thus originating a long line of scenic holocausts that led to Wagner and *Götterdämmerung* (see also *Ill.* 30).

29 (*below*) Lully's *Acis et Galathée* (1686), one of his most charming works, held the stage for many years. In this 1749 revival Madame de Pompadour (1721–64), Louis XV's mistress, is seen in the part of Galatea.

30 The designer for *Armide* was Jean Bérain (1637–1711). *Ill.* 28, showing the collapse of the palace, is taken from the cover of the score. *Ill.* 30 shows Bérain's design for the conflagration, on stage, in the last act.

to encourage the decorative side of the spectacle. Choruses, too, played a considerable part; as with the airs, their musical organization was simple, their massive homophony adding materially to the impression of dignity and grandeur.

The orchestra also, under Lully's brilliant direction, attained a hitherto unknown coherence, far outrunning the elementary usage of such a composer as Cavalli. The foundation was the string section, laid out in a solid five-voice structure; the *vingt-quatre violons du Roi*, soon to be imitated in London, set all Europe an example in ensemble and precision. Other instruments were added as occasion arose – oboes or flutes for pastoral scenes, trumpets and drums for fanfares and martial effects. The instrumental introduction acquired an increasing significance. Its two movements, the first slow, with characteristically arresting dotted rhythms, the second quicker, imitative or fully fugal, constitute the 'French overture' familiar in the music of Bach and

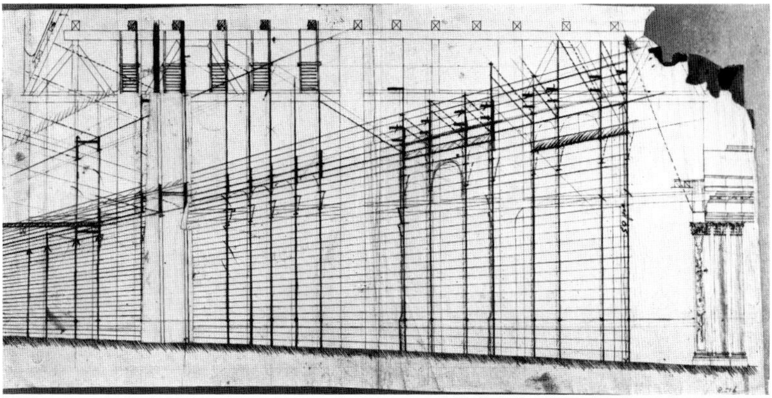

Handel. In the body of the opera the orchestra has already outgrown its function as a mere accompaniment, and its decorative-cum-illustrative role in, for example, Renaud's slumber in *Armide* is the prototype of later instances in the works of Handel, Rameau, Gluck and Mozart.

The visual presentation was as lavish as ever. Machines were the craze of the day, not only in opera, and Torelli's staging of *Andromède*, already mentioned, set the fashion for a whole series of such plays. They were given in a special theatre, known as the Salle des Machines,
32 built in 1660 in the Tuileries by yet another Italian, Gaspare Vigarani. His son, Carlo, worked with Lully as stage-designer, and was
30 followed by the first major French scenographer, Jean Bérain, whose costumes vied with those of the Italians in fantasy and extravagance.

The type of opera established in Paris by Lully, the expatriate Italian, differed in some essentials from that evolving in his native land; and not long after his death these differences provided the ammunition for the opening salvoes of a pamphlet war that was waged intermittently for close on a hundred years. The verbose and discursive *Parallèle des Italiens et des Français* of François Raguenet, championing the music of the Italians and published in 1702, was answered in 1704 by an equally lengthy vindication of the French style by Le Cerf de la Viéville – *Comparaison de la musique italienne et de la musique française*. Put in a nutshell, the differences are these. The French adopted the literary approach to drama, and argued that the

31 (*left*) Productions in the *Salle des machines* were continued in the eighteenth century by Servandoni (1695–1766). This illustration shows one of his working sketches, intended for Lully's *Atys*. Servandoni (more properly Servandony) was born at Lyons; he worked in many centres outside Paris, including Dresden, Stuttgart and London.

32 A scene by Carlo Vigarini for Lully's *Thesée* (1675), showing the elaborate costumes and headdresses in vogue at the time (cf. *Ill.* 26).

musical setting of words should be simple, following and reinforcing the natural inflexions of the voice and the cadences of the poetry. This, we have seen, was what Lully strove to do. The Italians, while conceding this as a point of departure (it had been after all the fundamental principle of the Florentine Camerata and the New Music), held that purely musical factors, such as melody, harmony, timbre and so on, had their own individual and sometimes overriding contribution to add to the sum total. It is a basic difference of opinion that has endured throughout the history of opera.

Another fundamental distinction between the French and the Italian approach to their serious opera lay in the choice of subjects, for while the Italians found inspiration in the great historical figures of the past, such as Alexander the Great, Ptolemy or Nero, it was a cardinal principle of the French theoreticians that real-life personages were not

suited to operatic presentation. In this as in so many other matters the precedent was firmly set by Lully, who drew his material either from mythology (*Phaéton*, 1683), the pastoral tradition (*Acis et Galathée*,
*29* 1686), or the chivalric literature of the Middle Ages (*Amadis*, 1684;
*8, 30* *Armide*, 1686). His example was followed by his successors, André Campra, Henri Desmarets and André Destouches, and the convention persisted at least until the time of Gluck, whose five important French operas are all based on mythological subjects.

The thirty-two stage works of Lully's most illustrious follower, Jean-Philippe Rameau (1683–1764), also fall into these categories, as we see from a glance at some of the titles: *Hippolyte et Aricie* (his first opera, 1733), *Castor et Pollux* (1737) and *Dardanus* (1739). Rameau is a composer sadly misunderstood and neglected today, nor has he ever found much favour outside France, where his operas are revived from time to time (*Les Indes Galantes* and *Dardanus* have been staged at the Paris Opéra). Elsewhere good modern recordings have revived interest in Rameau's works. He accepted happily the decorative form of opera laid down by Lully, with its *mélange* of spectacle, transformations, ballet (he even preserved the term *entrée*, borrowed from ballet proper, to signify acts or scenes), its pastorals and its 'imitation of nature'. But though the framework may have been old-fashioned the musical content was sufficiently up to date to disturb his audiences. Too learned, too dissonant, too noisy, they complained – charges that were later to be levelled against Mozart, Wagner and Schoenberg.

He was fifty before he wrote his first opera, and had already made a reputation as an organist, as a composer of church music and as the author of a treatise on harmony that was to have far-reaching consequences for the whole of musical thought. It is scarcely surprising that his operas reflect his seriousness of outlook. They are solidly built. His is not the charm of the facile, superficial melodist; his appeal is rather through the strength of his linear writing for both singers and orchestra, and through the richness and variety of his harmony. His scores were the fullest that had so far appeared in the opera house; in even the simplest dances the part-writing, far from being perfunctory, is engineered with loving care, while the airs afford a constant interplay between the voice and several independent instrument lines in the orchestra. The chorus, too, no longer restricted to simple homophony, has to take its part in the contrapuntal web. In short, Rameau demanded from his performers a *musical* intelligence as

33 In 1745 an entertainment was mounted at the palace at Versailles to celebrate the wedding of the dauphin with Maria Teresa of Spain. This was *La Princesse de Navarre*, by Voltaire, with music by Rameau. The occasion was commemorated by a series of engravings by Charles-Nicolas Cochin (1715–90). The orchestra has now been enlarged to about fifty players.

well as vocal ability and dramatic flair, and in this respect he stands as a forerunner of his immediate successor, Gluck, as well as of Mozart, Berlioz, Spontini and Wagner.

While all these somewhat formal theatrical entertainments were being enjoyed at the highest level, in the monarch's immediate circle, an absurd comedy of errors was being enacted below stairs. To understand what happened we must retrace our steps a little and

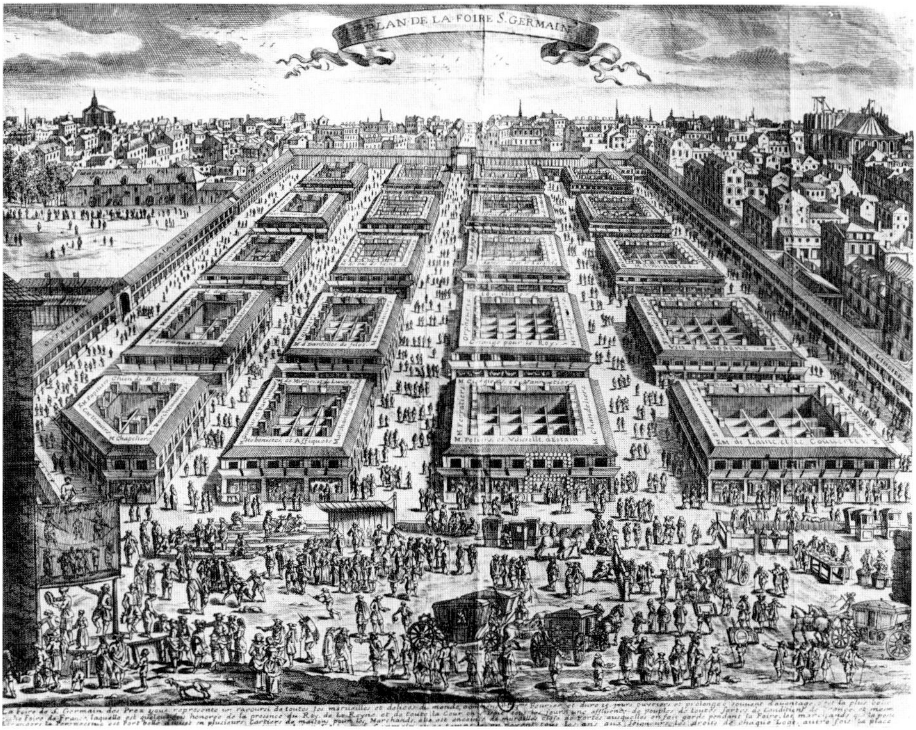


34 The Saint-Germain Fair in the sixteenth century. Rope dancers can be seen performing in a booth in the bottom left-hand corner of the picture.

examine the amusements and diversions open to the humbler citizens of the country.

Like every other medieval city Paris had its seasonal agricultural markets, the Fairs. Here livestock and merchandise of every kind were bought and sold; in the wake of this serious trading came the inevitable sideshows of fortune tellers, acrobats, singers, rope dancers, comedians and all manner of curiosities, all competing for the attention and the loose change of the crowds in holiday mood. Performances at first were in the open air, or in tents; gradually, and
*34, 35* especially at the more important fairs such as those at Saint-Laurent and Saint-Germain, more permanent booths began to be set up. By the sixteenth century the latter fair had developed into a covered market of considerable size.

35 A dramatic performance in progress in the open air at the Théâtre de la Foire, 1756, at the Saint-Laurent Fair.

The entertainments seem at first to have been harmless, if not very uplifting. But when in 1595 an attempt was made to replace the performing dogs or the dancing rats by plays with human actors, some unexpected difficulties arose. The Comédiens de l'Hôtel de Bourgogne had been granted the sole right to perform comedies in Paris, and naturally saw this new development as a threat to their monopoly. Their attempt to obtain an injunction restraining the Fair players was the first skirmish in a prolonged battle of wits that was not finally resolved until the middle of the eighteenth century.

The persistence with which the privileged companies (the Opéra, the Comédie-française, and the Comédie-italienne) sought to enforce their legal rights was matched by the ingenuity of the Fair players in circumventing them. Forbidden to act 'any spectacle where there is

dialogue', they resorted to monologue, one actor alone speaking, the others responding by mime and gesture. This provoked an ordinance forbidding speaking, in its turn to be countered by the Fair players who obtained permission from the Opéra (which held the monopoly) to sing and to use scenery. When even singing was denied them, they devised another ruse. If they could neither speak nor sing, what then? Why, play the scenes in dumb show; have the words of the songs written on placards, have the tunes played by the orchestra – there was nothing against that – and encourage the *audience* to sing.

Early in the eighteenth century the title *opéra-comique* appears for the first time. Scenes were still played mute, but the procedure was

36 (*left*) This print, no doubt somewhat stylized, shows not only the banner, or *écriteau*, carrying the words, and supported by the two *putti*, but includes a diminutive 'cloud machine' in the act of descent.

37 Le Jeu Royal de la Paulme: a tennis match in progress. These indoor tennis courts were much used, especially in France, for the performance of early operas. The oblong shape, with a gallery at the side for spectators, makes an interesting comparison with the grander premises illustrated earlier (*Ills* 24, 32).

refined by a system of *écriteaux*, which, according to Genest's history *36*
of L'opéra-comique, were 'a kind of linen "banner", on a roller, with the verses in large letters, and supplied with the name of the character singing them. This was lowered from the proscenium arch, carried by two children dressed as *putti* who unrolled the banner. The orchestra played the music of the couplets, the audience sang the couplets, while the actors mimed them.'

The *opéra-comique* achieved enormous popularity, especially when writers such as Fuzelier and Le Sage (the author of *Gil Blas*) began to collaborate. But even when in 1715 the theatre at the Saint-Germain Fair officially began the career of the French Opéra-comique as an operatic institution, the troubles were far from over. Indeed, it was nearly another forty years before the formal amalgamation on 3 February 1762 of the Opéra-comique with the Comédie-italienne finally resolved the differences and opened up the possibilities of a fuller and richer development.

In the meantime the Fair theatres had made a very positive contribution to the history of opera. In their *pièces en vaudevilles* – plays interspersed with songs sung to known melodies – they established the form taken over in England by Gay and Pepusch in *The Beggar's Opera* and by the German *Singspiel*; and in their *pièces à ariettes*, which originally parodied Italian arias by the substitution of French words, they paved the way for nineteenth-century operetta and Offenbach. They gave encouragement to lively writers such as Le Sage, Fuzelier, Orneval and Charles-Simon Favart, who later became director of the Opéra-comique and whose charming *Bastien et Bastienne* was set by the boy Mozart.

Another director was Jean Monnet, who took over and rebuilt the theatre in 1743, with new and more luxurious decor in which the
*38* painter François Boucher had a hand. With Monnet we are flung into the midst of the 'Querelle des Bouffons', the second major campaign in the Hundred Years Pamphlet War.

It was a performance of Pergolesi's *La Serva Padrona* ('The Maid as Mistress') at the Opéra in 1752 by a visiting Italian company that caused the Italophiles to reach for their pens. French, they argued, was an unsuitable language for music, and French composers were inept at setting it. (There was some excuse: *Le Devin du Village* ('The Village Soothsayer'), words and music by Jean-Jacques Rousseau, was amateurish.) Monnet was stung into action. Pretending to agree with this verdict, he put it about that, not finding a good enough musician in Paris, he had to scour the Continent to find an Italian composer with sufficient knowledge of the French language to set a French libretto. The result was *Les Troqueurs*, performed with brilliant success on 30 July 1753 in his fine new theatre. Only then did he reveal that, in fact, the *ariettes* were the work of a Frenchman, Antoine Dauvergne, a composer later associated with the Concerts Spirituels (an important series of concerts in Paris) and a future director of the Opéra.

Monnet, it is true, threw away this tactical advantage, if it really was one; perhaps he realized how hollow the whole discussion was. The librettist of *Les Troqueurs*, Jean Joseph Vade, died in 1757, and Monnet

38 François Boucher (1703–70), Madame de Pompadour's favourite artist, designed extensively for the Parisian theatres. He designed the scenery and costumes for Rameau's *Les Indes galantes*, as well as working in the 1750s for the theatres of the Saint-Germain and Saint-Laurent Fairs. Little of this work remains; the rustic landscape shown in the illustration is preserved in the Amiens Museum.

turned to Favart who, it may be, pressed the claims of a young Italian composer. This was Egidio Duni, whose setting of Favart's slight but charming *Ninette à la Cour* had been warmly welcomed in 1755 at Parma, then under a Francophile *régime*. On this being successfully repeated in Paris, Duni was persuaded to leave Parma and, with *Le Peintre Amoureux de son modèle*, produced at Monnet's theatre in 1757, began a sojourn in the French capital that ended only with his death. (France has a habit of absorbing foreign composers: Lully, Duni, Cherubini, Spontini, Meyerbeer, Offenbach are some of the more notable who have done the substantial, and usually best, part of their work in Paris.)

With Duni, who wrote about twenty operas for the Parisian stage, the Opéra-comique can fairly be said to have been launched as a

39 Rich costumes and ornate headdresses continued to be a feature of French theatrical style. A design by Boquet for Gossec's *Philémon et Baucis* (1775).

national institution; for the next hundred years the supply of writers and composers with the necessary qualities of deftness, wit and sentiment (not sentimentality) never dried up. Hard on the heels of Duni came Pierre Alexandre Monsigny (*Le Roi et le Fermier*, 1762; *Rose et Colas*, 1764; *Le Déserteur*, 1769); François André Danican Philidor (*Le Sorcier*, 1764; *Tom Jones*, 1765), and above all André Erneste Modeste Grétry, whose long list includes *Le Huron* (1768), *Le Tableau Parlant* (1769), *Les Deux Avares* (1770), *Zémire et Azore* (1771), *La Fausse Magie* (1775) and *Richard Cœur de Lion* (1784). Together with their librettists (Favart, Anseaume, Sedaine, Orneval, Marmontel, Marsollier, François-Benoît Hoffman) these composers fashioned a lyric theatre typically French in its elegance, its polish, its avoidance of rodomontade – an art which, for all its apparent fragility, crossed frontiers easily and was sufficiently robust to survive the cataclysm of the French Revolution.

## Opera in England from Purcell to Arne

In view of Great Britain's erratic operatic history it is ironic to reflect how near London was to having the first public opera house to be built outside Italy. In 1639 Sir William Davenant obtained a licence to erect a theatre wherein he might 'exercise musick, musical presentations, dancing, or any other the like'. Davenant, then Poet Laureate and an important figure in the theatre of the day, did not immediately carry out his intentions, perhaps because he was shrewd enough to sense the first signs of the impending Civil War. This, disrupting the country's musical life and closing the theatres at the very moment when opera was at such an exciting stage of its development in Italy, was an unmitigated disaster.

Amends were made after the Restoration in 1660, but some of the damage was irreparable. One of the most promising of the younger composers, William Lawes, was an unnecessary casualty of the war, killed accidentally during the siege of Chester in 1645. His elder brother Henry, whose music for Milton's *Comus* had won such high *41*
praise from the poet, and the much younger Matthew Locke, were both denied the full exercising of their considerable dramatic gifts by the restrictions of the Commonwealth.

This is all the more to be lamented since for once in England's history she had writers who were not only sympathetic to but knowledgeable about music. Music had permeated the Elizabethan stage, and since then much valuable experience in combined theatrical operations had been gained in the masques, devised in emulation of French and Italian models, though on the whole mounted with somewhat less extravagance.

Stemming from the royal entertainments under Elizabeth I, the masque reached its apogee during the reign of James I, from about 1605 to 1620. These courtly charades have vanished beyond hope of revival. The literary portions survive in quantity, by poets such as Thomas Campion, James Shirley and above all Ben Jonson, but the music, by Nicholas Laniere, Alfonso Ferrabosco, Thomas Campion

This designe I conceaue to bee fit for the inuention and
to add or alter any thing I desier to receaue hir
designe againe by this bearer. The collors allso
choise; but my oppinion is that seueral frosh greenes
siluer will be most propper /


40 The queen's costume; one of the designs by Inigo Jones (1573–1651) for the masque *Chloridia*, presented at the court in 1631.

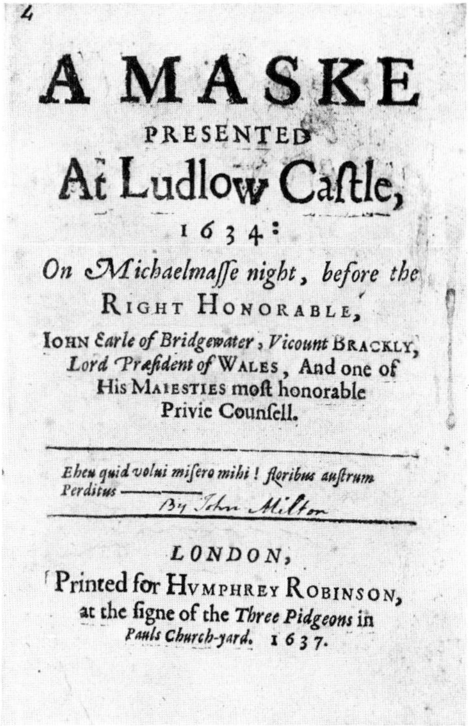
A MASKE
PRESENTED
At Ludlow Castle,
1634:
*On Michaelmasse night, before the*
RIGHT HONORABLE,
IOHN *Earle of Bridgewater, Vicount* BRACKLY,
*Lord Præsident of* WALES, And one of
His MAIESTIES most honorable
Privie Counsell.

*Eheu quid volui misero mihi! floribus austrum
Perditus* ——

LONDON,
Printed for HVMPHREY ROBINSON,
at the signe of the *Three Pidgeons* in
*Pauls Church-yard.* 1637.

41 Though described as a 'maske', Milton's *Comus* leans more towards the type of pastoral opera. The initiative for the work probably came from Henry Lawes, who was a friend of Milton; they had worked together on a similar project a year or two before.

and the Lawes brothers, exists only in fragments, if at all. That written by Henry Lawes for *Comus* is woefully incomplete; other dances and airs, mostly unidentified, are preserved in the form of lute transcriptions. The loss of Laniere's music to Ben Jonson's *Lovers made Men* (1617) is particularly to be deplored since, according to Jonson himself, 'the whole masque was sung after the Italian maner, *stilo recitativo*'. Laniere was a man of parts, for he also painted the scenery; he was later commissioned by Charles I to buy pictures from Italy for the royal Collection.

Something of the splendour of the productions can be recaptured by studying the lively and imaginative drawings by Inigo Jones, *40*
preserved at Chatsworth in Derbyshire. Jones visited Italy in 1613–14 (he may have been there earlier), and returned to England fired with enthusiasm for Italian stage technique, but even before that time his sketches, particularly for costumes, display a riotous fancy that anticipates the work of Jean Bérain.

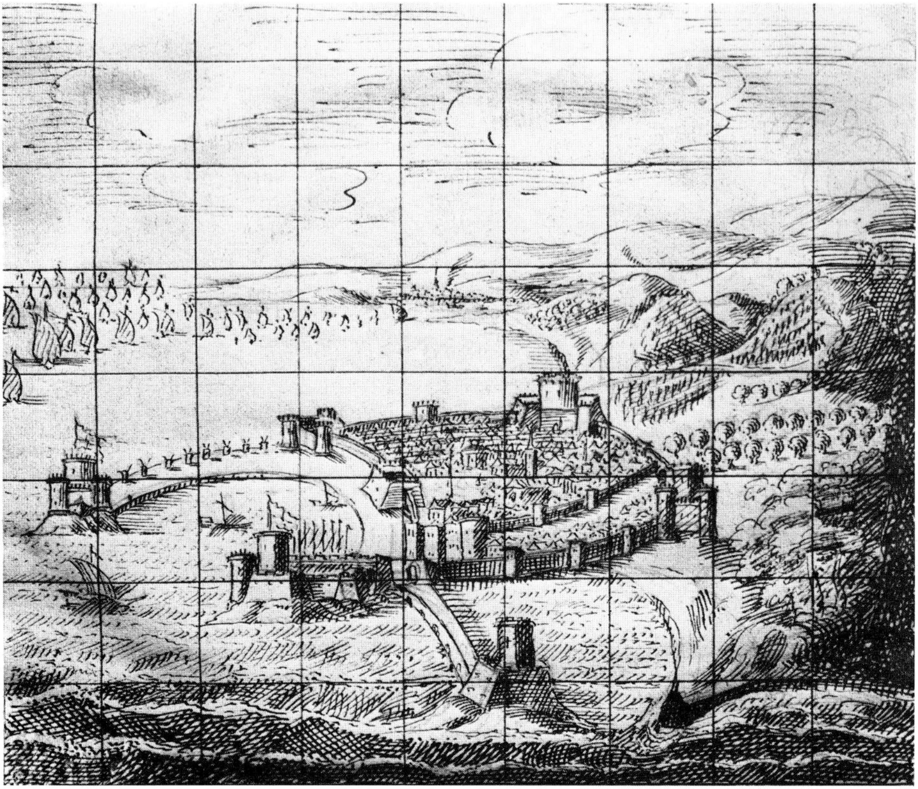

Jones lived too early to have any direct influence on the operatic stage and it was left to his co-worker and successor, John Webb, to design the scenery for what is described with some truth as the first opera ever to be produced in England, *The Siege of Rhodes*. The date was 1656 – four years before the Restoration; the place was Rutland House, in Charterhouse Yard, on a very small improvised stage (the public theatres were still closed). It was presented by the author, Davenant, who described it, not indeed as an 'opera', but as 'A Representation by the art of Prospective in Scenes and the Story sung in Recitative Musick'. The composers were Henry Lawes, Matthew Locke and the Royalist Captain Cooke who at the Restoration was called upon to rehabilitate the music in Westminster Abbey. Henry Purcell, the father of the composer, was one of the performers. The piece was revived once or twice but the music is lost.

*42, 43*

42, 43 *Left:* Design for a backcloth by John Webb (1611–72) for the first performance in 1656 of *The Siege of Rhodes*. The work was revived in 1661, for the opening of the new theatre in Lincoln's Inn Fields, when Thomas Betterton (*c.* 1635–1710) played the part of Solimano (*right*).

In his very full discussion of the work in *Foundations of English Opera*, Edward J. Dent points to some of its unique features, for example the rejection of classical mythology in favour of an historical event as recent as the siege of Rhodes by the Turks in 1522. It is worth remarking, too, that it antedates by many years the first of Lully's true operas; the French influence came later, in the wake of the Restoration. Webb's scenes were merely painted backcloths, miniatures of what Davenant had seen in Paris (he was there when Corneille's *Andromède* was given) and what he hoped to see realized in England when times were better and his new theatre was built.

Davenant died in 1668 and so never saw his handsome new Dorset 44
Garden theatre, which opened its doors in 1671. Built in the modern style with a proscenium arch, it was well equipped backstage, and over the next two decades played a major part in London's theatrical

44 The Dorset Garden theatre, seen here, was in Blackfriars, on the site of the present City of London Boys' School. Designed and built by Sir Christopher Wren, it cost £10,000. It was the most resplendent theatre that England had yet seen, with a gilt proscenium arch decorated with carvings by Grinling Gibbons.

life. Though it was not strictly an opera house, some of the versions, or perversions, of Shakespeare by Shadwell and others performed there spill over into the regions of opera by virtue of the music provided for them by Purcell (1659–95).

One of the works played at the Dorset Garden theatre in 1673 was Shadwell's *Psyche*, patterned on the *comédie-ballet* of the same name produced by Molière and Lully in 1671. The music was shared between Locke, who wrote the songs, and an Italian, Giovanni Battista Draghi, who provided the instrumental music. Locke's share survives because he had it published; Dent, who printed some of it in *Foundations of English Opera*, felt the music to be less satisfying than Locke's earlier contribution to Shirley's masque, *Cupid and Death* (1653), but remarks that Shadwell fuses the play, the machines and the music 'into a whole, almost in the Wagner manner, all three arts uniting to produce an effect such as none could achieve by itself'.

How assured composers had become in handling 'Recitative Musick' is demonstrated in a delightful pastoral, described as a masque, but really an opera in miniature, *Venus and Adonis*, by John Blow. This was written for Charles II, and performed at court by one of his mistresses, Mary Davis, and her daughter, who, if the date now accepted for performance is correct, was only nine years old. It is Blow's only essay for the stage, and lay neglected until it was revived by Rutland Boughton at Glastonbury in 1920.

If this seems to be dalliance in the byways rather than the highroad of opera, what shall we say to a tragedy, written for schoolgirls, played in a village by the Thames? Children's operas are almost a commonplace today, after the example set by Hindemith with *Wir bauen eine Stadt* ('We build a City', 1931); how many dare we put beside this masterpiece from seventeenth-century England? The opera was *Dido and Aeneas*, music by Henry Purcell, libretto by Nahum Tate, and it 46
was performed by the young ladies of Mr Josias Priest's school in Chelsea – and that is about all we know of the circumstances surrounding it. Purcell's autograph score is lost; we do not know exactly when the work was produced, but it was apparently in the year 1689; nor do we know precisely where, though Dennis Arundell in *The Critic at the Opera* has put forward arguments that it was played in the open air, possibly in the Wood Yard adjacent to Priest's school in Gorges House.

Whatever reservations one might have about *Psyche* or *The Siege of Rhodes*, or about those plays which, as the seventeenth-century gossip Roger North says, 'were called Operas but had bin more properly styled Semioperas', there is no disputing *Dido's* claim to the title 'opera'. Though small in scale, lasting barely an hour and, as befits a school opera, not too taxing on its performers, it is sung throughout, to music beside which that of Purcell's contemporaries sounds contrived and constrained. It is his contribution alone that breathes life into the piece, whether it is the sailors' carousals, the witches' incantations or Dido's grief. Her final lament is one of the unassailable masterpieces of music; it and the poignant choral elegy which concludes the opera testify in the most moving way to the viability of opera in English.

*Dido* ushered in an astonishing period of creativity. In six years Purcell provided music for some forty plays, and in at least five instances his share was substantial enough for them to be considered at

45 A scene from the English Opera Group's 1971 production of Purcell's *King Arthur*, Sadler's Wells theatre.

46 Henry Purcell, from the portrait, formerly attributed to Godfrey Kneller, in the National Portrait Gallery, London.

least as 'Semioperas'. The first of these was *Dioclesian*, produced at Dorset Garden in June 1690. This was less an opera than a heroic play garnished with music, dancing, pageantry and scenic transformations. The climax of the work came in the last act, a brilliant masque in which Purcell had the lion's share. Its successor in the following year, *King Arthur or The British Worthy*, moved somewhat closer to the 45
operatic ideal. But though its author, John Dryden – one of the few distinguished English men of letters to give the operatic problem any serious consideration – described it as a 'dramatic opera', it is so only within the conventions of the seventeenth-century English stage. The main characters do not sing, but speak their lines; thus Purcell was deprived of one of the most potent weapons in the opera composer's armoury, characterization through song. The same handicap is present in two Shakespearean concoctions of his last years, *The Fairy Queen* (based on *A Midsummer Night's Dream*) and *The Tempest.*

So Purcell, for all his sublime musical genius and his superb dramatic instinct, remained a might-have-been in the history of opera, a victim of circumstances. The high hopes he expressed, in the Preface to *Dioclesian* – 'Musick is but yet in its Nonage, a forward Child, which gives hope of what it may be hereafter in England, when the Masters of it shall find more Encouragement' – were dashed when his untimely death in 1695 at the age of thirty-five left a great gap to be filled.

GEORGE FRIDERIC

The aim of both Dryden and Purcell had been the establishment of serious opera in English. To this end Purcell in the 1680s made a close study of all the Italian music he could get hold of, but adapted the new 'recitative' style to his native language, with marvellous success. He never set one word of Italian, and both he and Dryden would have been appalled and outraged by the Italian invasion of the next fifty years.

The take-over was gradual. Even before the turn of the century the vogue for Italian singers was beginning. Then adaptations of popular Venetian successes began to appear, first in translations, later, as at Hamburg, with imported Italians singing in their own language, the other parts being performed in English. But London had seen very few all-Italian operas before Handel's *Rinaldo*, in 1711.

Handel as a composer stood head and shoulders above all the others working in the *opera seria* tradition (discussed in Chapter Five), and it is one of the ironies of operatic history that his achievements should have made so little impression on the course of that history. Because his area of activity was London, to all intents and purposes an operatic backwater, his works were unknown in the main centres of Italian opera. Like Purcell he worked without the artistic and financial support of a court; instead the opera was run by a group of wealthy amateurs who suffered under the delusion that opera could be made profitable, yet squandered their resources by paying out exorbitant sums to foreign singers in a vain attempt to maintain a 'star' system. Yet despite it all, this amazing man dominated the London lyric stage for thirty years with a series of thirty-five operas in a style, format and language alien to the traditions of his adopted country, where public opinion was often indifferent and occasionally hostile. 47

Conscious perhaps of the peculiar problems of his situation, Handel and his librettists (principally Nicola Haym and Paolo Rolli) covered a wider range than the court composers usually did. He set only two texts by the universally admired court poet Metastasio (*Poro*, 1731; *Ezio*, 1732) and wrote only a few 'historical' operas (*Giulio Cesare*, 1724; *Tolomeo*, 1728), but chose a variety of other themes. There were

47 George Frederick Handel, from an engraving on the published score of his oratorio, *Alexander's Feast* (1738).

48, 49 An engraving by William Hogarth (1697–1764), 'Masquerades and Operas', satirizing the vogue for 'foreign' opera, and showing the plays of Ben Jonson and Shakespeare relegated to the dustbin. The opera advertised on the banner is Handel's *Flavio* (1723), a scene from which is reproduced below. The singers are the castrato Senesino, the soprano Cuzzoni, and the castrato Berenstadt.

50 Joan Sutherland in the title role of Handel's *Alcina*, in Franco Zeffirelli's production at Covent Garden, London, 1960–61.

pastoral operas (*Il Pastor fido*, 1712; *Atalanta*, 1736) and 'magic' operas (*Orlando*, 1733; *Alcina*, 1735). *Serse* (1738) was adapted from an old 50
text by Nicolò Minato that Cavalli had previously set; other librettists drawn on were Quinault (*Teseo*, 1713), Antonio Salvi (*Rodelinda*, 1725), Apostolo Zeno (*Scipione*, 1726) and Mateo Noris (*Sosarme*, 1732).

Structurally these are 'aria' operas, following a pattern that had been established by Neapolitan composers such as Alessandro Scarlatti (1660–1725) and Handel's contemporary Nicola Porpora (1686–1768). The main musical interest of such operas resides in the arias; these, akin to the soliloquy of spoken drama, tend to exploit situations and emotional states, but in the hands of a dramatic composer of Handel's stature could also play their part in delineating character.

51 A satire on *The Beggar's Opera*, by Hogarth.

Writing as comparatively recently as 1912, it was possible for a distinguished English music critic, H. C. Colles, to state that 'it would be difficult, if not impossible, to make any one of Handel's operas tolerable to a modern audience'. This reflected the general nineteenth-century attitude that these works, stuffed though they are with fine music, dramatically belonged to an extinct species. This was a by-product of the doctrine that Gluck had reformed *opera seria* out of existence. However, during the past fifty years, more and more of Handel's operas have been staged and recorded, and it is now seen that the 'credibility gap' is not as wide as was supposed. Given intelligent production, good singing and a knowledge of eighteenth-century musical style and theatre convention, these works come vividly to life as one aspect of the musico-dramatic entity we call opera, as valid and enjoyable theatrical experiences.

52 Lucy Lockit (left) and Polly Peachum (right) entreating their fathers, the gaoler and the informer, to save Macheath's life. A painting by Hogarth, who executed several versions of this scene from Act III of *The Beggar's Opera*.

It is true that the conventions of *opera seria* struck some people as absurd even in Handel's own day, and even in the country of its origin. For example, in about 1720, in Venice, the composer Benedetto Marcello published a pamphlet, *Il Teatro alla Moda*, in which operatic abuses and excesses were held up to ridicule. English critics included Joseph Addison, possibly a trifle soured by the failure of his own Italian-style opera, *Rosamund* (1707); and in 1728 the satire was given a practical form on the stage of Lincoln's Inn Fields theatre, when John Gay and John Christopher Pepusch turned the operatic world topsy-turvy with *The Beggar's Opera* and opened wide a doorway to a new kind of musical entertainment that has survived until our own times. It was technically a 'ballad' opera; that is, Gay's words were linked to tunes previously composed. It was thus similar to the *pièces en vaudeville* of Paris mentioned earlier. *51, 52*

53 Richard Leveridge (*c.* 1670–1758), a bass, and one of the finest English singers of his day. He was also a composer. He sang in several of Handel's operas (*Il Pastor fido*, 1712; *Teseo*, 1713) and was a popular figure at Vauxhall and Ranelagh Gardens.

54 (*right*) Mrs Farrell and Charles Reinhold as Artaxerxes and Artabanes in Thomas Arne's *Artaxerxes*. If the engraving is true to life, the domestic, bourgeois quality of the set is in marked contrast to the English set shown in *Ill.* 49, and to the even more elaborate and gorgeous scenes in Continental *opera seria* (*Ills* 55, 56).

*The Beggar's Opera* did not kill Italian opera in England, nor did it even spell Handel's downfall, some of his best works, such as *Orlando*, *Ariodante*, *Alcina* and *Serse*, being written after 1728. Its phenomenal success in fact turned attention to another Handel work to Gay's words, the charming *Acis and Galatea*, originally written in 1718 and revived frequently from 1731, sometimes with Handel's approval, sometimes without. Its various titles – Serenata, Masque, Pastoral – are less revealing than Gay's 1732 description of it as an 'English Pastoral Opera'. It is Handel's only stage work written in English; listening to the tender, delicate treatment of the love between Acis and Galatea, the apt characterization of the galumphing giant Polyphemus, the sensitivity of the chorus work and the subtlety of the orchestration, one realizes what a glorious chapter on opera in English failed to get written through Handel's pursuance of the *opera seria* ideal. Eventually, changing public taste, and the increasing cost and other practical difficulties of production, forced Handel to abandon Italian opera for English oratorio, of which he became the supreme master. Among his late oratorios are a few secular works (such as *Semele*, 1744, set to a libretto by William Congreve), which have been successfully performed on the stage in our day, and indeed some of the oratorios (such as *Saul* and *Samson*) that draw on Biblical subjects have shown that their inherent sense of drama can be brought fully alive in the opera house.

Of the native composers at this time the one with the most individual voice was Thomas Augustine Arne (1710–78). His talents were not wide or deep enough for him to succeed in fully-fledged Italianate opera, though he tried. His most successful venture in this field was *Artaxerxes* (1762), in English, to his own translation of Metastasio; two soprano arias from this work lingered on well into the nineteenth century. His true gifts, however, lay in a lighter vein, in comedies and rustic pieces such as *Thomas and Sally* (1760) or *Love in a* 54

*Village* (1762). The librettist of these was Isaac Bickerstaffe, who also wrote a number of plays for which Charles Dibdin provided music, among them *Love in the City* (1767) and *The Padlock* (1768), based on Cervantes. Besides Bickerstaffe the librettists included some weightier names such as the novelist Henry Fielding, who wrote a number of ballad operas in the 1730s, and whose *Tom Jones* was the basis of Philidor's opera; and Richard Brinsley Sheridan, whose *The Duenna*, produced originally in 1775 with music by the Linleys, father and son, has also provided operatic material in this century for Prokofiev (1946) and Roberto Gerhard (1948). Other composers include William Boyce (*The Chaplet*, 1749); Samuel Arnold (*The Maid of the Mill*, 1765); William Shield (his *Rosina*, 1782, has been recorded); and Stephen Storace, whose sister, Nancy, was the first Susanna in *Figaro* in 1786, and whose greatest success was probably the pastiche *No Song, no Supper* (1790).

Indeed, throughout the eighteenth century there was no lack of demand in London and other cities for comic opera. Over a hundred ballad operas were produced in the ten years following *The Beggar's Opera*, and Eric Walter White, in *The Rise of English Opera*, making no claim to completeness, lists 114 or so between 1738 and 1800. Summing up, we can say that Britain's contribution to the somewhat patchy field of eighteenth-century comic opera was not negligible. Like the *Singspiel* in Germany and the *opéra-comique* in France, these works were less operas than plays with added music: charming, piquant music, written with taste and skill, but doing little more dramatically than add details to a character or a situation already made clear in the libretto. The general level was not below that of Italy or Germany, if we set aside the work of one man. It is the effulgence of Mozart that has dimmed the light of all his contemporaries, of whatever country.

# Opera Seria. The Court Opera

*Opera seria* is, as it were, the 'piano nobile' of the eighteenth-century operatic palace. The stately proportions, the dignified formality, graced with arabesques that are themselves formalized, furnished an ornate counterpoint to the stylized living that the courts enjoyed. The elaborate stage sets devised by the Bibienas, Juvarras and Galliaris simply continued their splendid architecture on to the stage; the solid columns, arches and porticoes flowed uninterruptedly, imperceptibly merging into their painted lath-and-plaster counterfeit. The proscenium arch was less a barrier than a corner, round which one seemed to glimpse another wing or colonnade of the vast palace; the eye was guided by the *scena per angolo*, the diagonal settings introduced about the year 1700 by Ferdinando Bibiena. The illusion was fostered by the lighting, which was hardly more brilliant on the stage than in the auditorium, where house lights remained lit during the performances. The setting was in reality the entire theatre; emperor, prince, king or duke, with their courtiers, apparelled as richly as the actors on stage, were an essential part of the show.

Such an opera house, palatial within the exact meaning of the term, became during the eighteenth century an indispensable luxury at all the courts in Europe. In it the autocratic dictator could see his idealized benevolent despotism at work; Alexander the Great, resolute in war, magnanimous in victory, or Titus, removed, god-like, far above petty jealousy, and extending an almost more than Christian forbearance and forgiveness towards those who had plotted against him, reflected a burnished if exaggerated image of the princely qualities each ruler saw himself as possessing.

*Opera seria* required for its fullest flowering the ambience of a rich, self-centred autocratic court, with a ruler vain or insecure enough to welcome sycophantic flattery. This partly explains Handel's difficulties in London, where *opera seria* was offered, not to a self-admiring court but to a public that had already moved on to the next stage of political awareness.

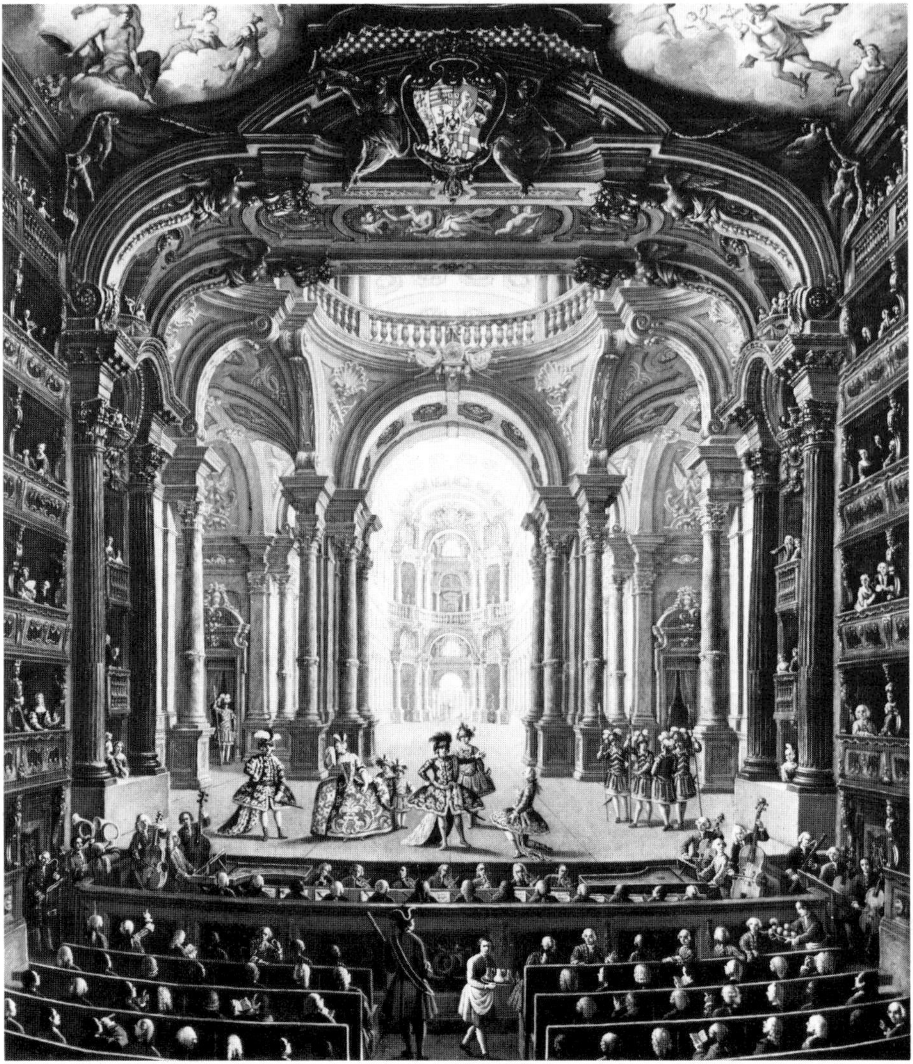

55 A performance in the Teatro Regio, Turin, 1740. The orchestra can be seen exceptionally clearly.

56 (*right*) A *scena per angolo* (at an angle, instead of the central perspective shown in *Ill.* 55), by Francesco Bibiena (1659–1739), dated 1703.

Diseggno del novo teatro aperto nell' anno 1703. nell' Accademia dell' Ill.mi SS.ri Ardenti al Porto diretto dalli RR.PP. Somaschi
epitura del celebre Sig. Francesco Bibiena Bolognese
Carlo Antonio Buffagnotti Fr.

The circumstances in which the court opera was written encouraged a stereotyped, safe approach, but in other conditions composers were emboldened to take a more adventurous line. The first historical
16 opera was Monteverdi's *The Coronation of Poppea*, in 1642. Since the work was given before a citizens' audience in the Republic of Venice, and there was no hieratical ruler to flatter, Monteverdi and his librettist, Busenello, could concentrate on a fine dramatic story with no fear of political or moral pressure. Poppea, a scheming harlot, makes her way into Nero's bed and on to the Empress's throne, kicking aside her own husband and Nero's lawful wife in the process. In dealing with those who have plotted against either him or Poppea, Nero shows no magnanimity, and the one person who shows awareness of the dignity and responsibilities of kingship, Seneca, is forced to commit suicide. Virtue, in short, does not triumph. But the characters are all human beings, not puppets; even the minor figures, such as Drusilla and Ottone, are rounded and alive. Nor is the plot without humour – a quality rigidly excluded from the court opera, but a frequent ingredient at Venice.

The composers following Monteverdi who satisfied Venice's thirst
17 for opera included Cavalli and Marc'Antonio Cesti. The former wrote some forty operas. Drawn in the main from mythological sources or from ancient pseudo-history, the plots abounded in complications, often, as in *La Costanza di Rosimonda* (1659), anticipating the intrigues of later Neapolitan opera. There were pastoral scenes, and abundant opportunites for machines and magical transformations. The music, always sincere and noble, could, under the inspiration of a fine libretto such as Busenello's *Didone abbandonata* (1641), reach an eloquence comparable to Purcell's. Nowhere does Cavalli freeze into the stiffness of court opera. The Venetians enjoyed humour, they appreciated pageantry and colour, they responded to good singing; above all they liked their entertainments to entertain.

57 Cesti's *Il Pomo d'Oro* ('The Golden Apple') has eclipsed his other operas in fame, if not necessarily in excellence. Like several Venetian composers he had connections with Vienna, and *Il Pomo d'Oro*, a court opera, was written for that city in 1666 for the wedding of Emperor Leopold I and the Infanta Margherita, thus recalling the origins of opera and the splendours of Medici weddings, which it outdid in opulence and extravagance. The sets, twenty-three in number and of unparalleled magnificence, were by the architect Lodovico Burnacini,

57, 58 One of the twenty-three designs by Lodovico Burnacini (1636–1707) for Cesti's *Pomo d'Oro*, Vienna, 1666, and (*below*) the interior of the theatre during the performance of *Il Pomo d'Oro*.

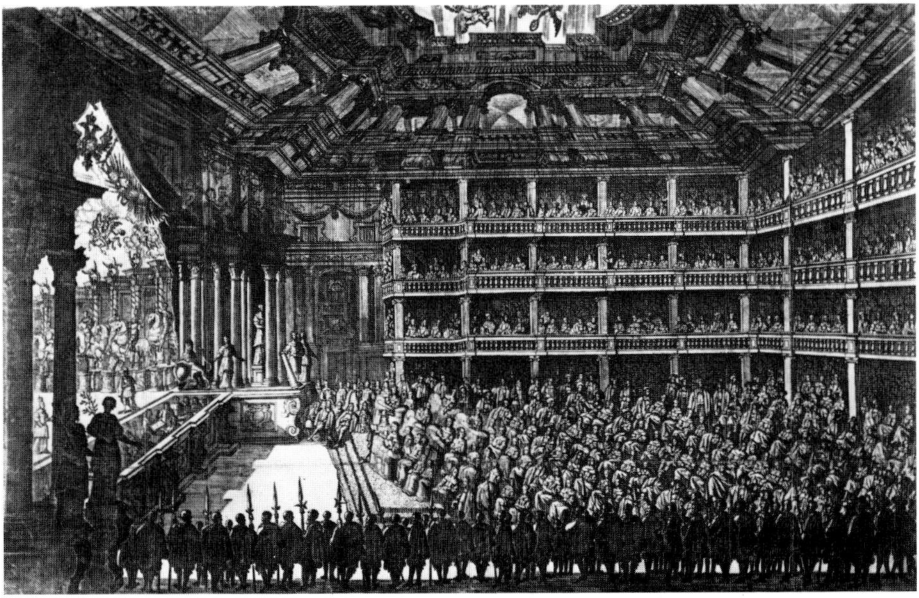

a name of paramount importance in the field of theatre decoration.
58 The theatre in which the work was presented, designed and built by him, was among the earliest of the resplendent chain of baroque theatres that was soon to spread across Europe from Lisbon to Leningrad.

If in this work, described as a *festa teatrale*, the balance between drama and music was upset by the too lavish spectacle, it was not long before another imbalance was created. The original conception of the 'New Music' had envisaged *stilo recitativo* as declaimed speech: no more. Then when, as for example in Orfeo's 'Possente spirto', Monteverdi had encouraged embellishments in the singer's part, these had arisen entirely from the dramatic requirements. But on the whole the vocal line of the mid-seventeenth century, as it is in Monteverdi, Cavalli, Cesti or Lully, remains simple. Though the operas themselves may have been forgotten, the limpid grace and suave contours of these arias have been familiar to generations of singers through the *Arie antiche* and the other vocal collections; they are the foundations on which a *bel canto* style is built.

The change of style associated with the rise of the north Italian violin school in the 1680s has already been noted (see page 30). This development, seen clearly in the arias of Alessandro Scarlatti, and even more marked in the work of the next generation of composers such as Handel or Bononcini, received a further impetus when Italian singers evolved voices rivalling the violin in agility, the trumpet in sonority and the organ in staying power. These were the *castrati* or male sopranos and contraltos who, appearing first in church choirs (Siface made his reputation thus before he went on the stage), soon came to dominate the theatre. Much, perhaps too much, has been made of their baleful influence. They have been castigated for being egocentric, vain, stupid, greedy; some no doubt were. Several, for example
59, 49 Farinelli, Senesino and Caffarelli, amassed large fortunes; so have other performers in their day and ours. They were not all stupid; Nicolini, who sang Rinaldo in Handel's opera of that name, was an extremely intelligent actor who won praise even from the prejudiced Addison; Porpora, composer, linguist, the most distinguished singing teacher in Europe, was esteemed by Handel, Hasse and Haydn, and the last-named even had some composition lessons from him.

Porpora was a Neapolitan, and under him Naples consolidated a reputation for singing that persisted well into the nineteenth century.

59 Carlo Broschi, known as Farinelli (1705–82), the most famous of all the castrati. His first appearance in London was with Handel's rivals, The Opera of the Nobility, founded in 1733 by the Prince of Wales's party in opposition to the king's party. They gave operas by Porpora, Hasse, Duni and others, and even one by Handel, *Ottone*, in 1734.

Opera had taken root there in the mid-seventeenth century, imported from Venice: like the Venetians, the Neapolitans preferred liveliness to solemnity, and their great contribution to opera's history lies in comedy. Scarlatti, for example, who had learnt his trade in Rome, preserved a comic element in many of the serious operas he wrote for Naples. But his main contributions were musical: the development of the 'Italian' overture (quick, slow, quick), later to be the basis of the symphony; the stabilization of the ternary form aria, A, B, A: and the emancipation of the siciliana dance form (he was a native Sicilian).

60 Design by Burnacini for Antonio Draghi's *Il Fuoco eterno* (1674).

The court type of *opera seria* was seen at its most characteristic in Vienna, at the court of Leopold I and his consort, and the Italian domination established then endured to the time of Beethoven and after. The chief composer associated with Vienna at this stage was
*60* Antonio Draghi. He moved there from Venice in 1682, became court composer, and over a period of some forty years produced a large quantity of operas and other theatrical entertainments. The libretti, in Italian as a matter of course, were largely supplied by the court poet, also Venetian, Count Minato.

Leopold's successors, Joseph I, Charles I and the Empress Maria Theresa, all subscribed to the view that imperial dignity was enhanced by the encouragement of learning and the arts. Italy continued to be pillaged for court poets, in the persons of Apostolo Zeno (1668–1750),
*61, 62* another Venetian, and Pietro Trapassi, known as Metastasio (1698–1782), who succeeded Zeno in his official capacity in 1729. Both were remarkable men, well above the common run of professional

61 Pietro Trapassi (1698–1782), better known as Metastasio. Most of his thirty or so libretti were set scores of times, sometimes more than once by the same composer.

62 A sketch by Fabrizio Galliari (1709–90) for Metastasio's *Olimpiade*, Turin, 1765 (composer unknown).

librettists. Zeno was a scholar who busied himself annotating and editing classical texts, as happy in his study as in the theatre. Metastasio was revered in his own day as a poet fit to be mentioned in the same breath as the famous names of Italy's past. He had great fluency, and had originally attracted notice by his extempore versification. He also had some talent as a composer. His letters, especially those to his *gemelle* (twin), as he calls him, Farinelli, besides being valuable for the insight they offer into his thoughts on the problems of music drama, reveal him as a man of equable and friendly disposition, with an unsuspected sense of humour.

Zeno and Metastasio largely settled the form of eighteenth-century court opera; their texts, in an easy flowing and elegant Italian, were set over and over again. The main argument was sustained in dialogue, set in *recitativo secco*, that is to say, supported by the harpsichord and cello only, in the characteristic baroque 'continuo' style; at emotional climaxes this expanded into 'accompanied' recitative, the strings of the orchestra joining in. Every now and then the quasi-prose blank verse would burgeon into short, rhymed lyrics which gave the composer the opportunity to provide some more expansive music – the arias or, more rarely, duets, in which the performers were likewise encouraged to display *their* creative powers in extemporized ornaments and variations. (It was this element, so jealously guarded by the singers, that was ultimately to prove one of the greatest weaknesses of the *opera seria*.) The *dramatis personae* were the heroes of antiquity, of noble rank, and as such the only actors cast for singing parts; their retinue (train-bearers, soldiers, servants) were silent, and sharply differentiated from the singers by dress, deportment and position on the stage.

These main characters (usually about four, with perhaps another couple playing subsidiary roles, as confidants or counsellors) were most often depicted as being in some amatory quandary of the type A loves B, B loves C, C loves A (or D); instances of mistaken identity are frequent, slaves or prisoners of war turning out to be of royal blood, and hence eligible in the marriage market. The nub of the drama lay, not so much in any physical conflict on- or off-stage (violence on-stage, though present in Shakespeare, remained on the whole taboo, as in Greek drama, until the nineteenth century), but rather in a moralistic struggle between love and duty. The A B A aria form was a tailor-made vehicle for posing the two sides of the argument; it came

63 *Costanza e Fortezza* ('Constancy and Fortitude'), music by Fux, decor (including the specially built auditorium for 4,000 spectators) by Giuseppe Bibiena (1696–1757). There were 100 instrumentalists and 200 singers.

in various stock patterns, *aria cantabile*, *aria di bravura*, *aria parlante*, and so on, to cover every situation.

In Vienna the principal Metastasian composers were the Italian Antonio Caldara, and his German contemporary, Johann Joseph Fux. Fux, known to all musicians as the author of the most famous counterpoint treatise ever written, *Gradus ad Parnassum*, became *Kapellmeister* to the Viennese court in 1715. His operas include the brilliant *Alcina* (1716), staged on a lake in the grounds of the Imperial Palace, and *Costanza e Fortezza*, also in the open, at Prague for the coronation of 63
Charles VI as Emperor in 1723. Another splendid centre was the Saxon court at Dresden, and here Johann Hasse, German but trained in Italy, was in command for about thirty years; his wife, Faustina Bordoni, was one of the greatest sopranos of the day. Agostino

64 The interior of the Residenztheater, Munich, built by Jean François de Cuvilliés (1698–1767). Damaged during the Second World War, it was restored and reopened in 1958.

65 (*right*) The interior of Giuseppe Bibiena's opera house at Bayreuth, built in 1748.

Steffani worked at Munich, while in Berlin another Italianate German, Karl Heinrich Graun, became Frederick the Great's *Kapellmeister* in 1740. Like Handel he ranged outside the narrow Zeno/Metastasio choice of subjects, his works including a *Rodelinda* (1741) and a *Montezuma* (1755).

In however favourable a light eighteenth-century *opera seria* is presented, it remains true that considerable adjustment is demanded of present-day audiences before they can begin to enjoy it. The parts for male soprano and contralto will always be a vexing problem. One of the hardest things for us to understand is the contemporary acceptance, apparently with complete equanimity, of the incongruity of passionate protestations of love from eunuchs incapable of its full consummation. Were they simply regarded as symbols, figures with no more reality than the make-believe grandeur of the scenic

background? If so, we can find justification for playing them as travesty roles instead of adopting the octave transposition to men's voices, which upsets the musical balance. The question of extemporization is no longer troublesome, at least in theory, and we can nowadays readily accept Pier Tosi's point of view when, in his *Observations on Florid Song*, he objects to singers 'having the Graces set down in Writing' on the ground that 'whoever accustoms himself to have Things put in his Mouth, will have no Invention, and becomes a Slave to his Memory'.

Then, too, we are so accustomed to the orchestra's major part in the total presentation that for the brunt to be borne by the singers on the stage seems an unnecessary deprivation. But this is an over-simplification. The eighteenth-century listener would have been reluctant to accept the Wagnerian and post-Wagnerian view of the orchestra's dominance, but he was already familiar with the instrumental depiction of thunder, lightning, storms, shipwrecks, the Elysian Fields, the Underworld, tranquil garden scenes, and the like. He could have seen the Wolf's Glen scene in *Der Freischütz*, with its preponderance of orchestral interest, as a valid extension of eighteenth-century practice – though he would, as usual, have complained that it was too noisy.

Orchestras grew in size, in both numbers of players and diversity of instruments. The small Lully string orchestra yielded to the Rameau orchestra of strings plus flutes, oboes and bassoons, with trumpets and drums for fanfares and jubilation. Horns found a footing in the orchestra, at first for hunting scenes; then they were gradually absorbed into the general texture. Trombones began to be used, but for solemnity rather than power; the contemporary trombone was a more soft-toned instrument than its modern counterpart. The clarinet was not commonly used until the last decades of the century, and even then not universally. It featured in the Paris Opéra from about 1770, but it was left to Mozart to realize fully its potentialities. His use of clarinets to illustrate the languishing, lovelorn ladies in *Così fan tutte* is exquisite, while his employment of the low, *chalumeau* register in his last opera, *La Clemenza di Tito*, provided a model for all subsequent composers.

The Metastasian *opera seria* began to come under really serious fire from about 1750. The controversy involved Italian, French, German and British writers; it laboured principles of aesthetics, invoking the

66 Francesco Algarotti (1712–64), writer and intellectual, born in Venice. He was a friend of Voltaire, Canaletto and Tiepolo. He collected paintings, was an art critic, and, besides writing on the aesthetics of opera, wrote a valuable essay on painting.

sacred name of Aristotle and embarking on pedantic discussions of the 'unities' and the 'imitation of nature'. There were heated arguments as to the rival merits of the two main styles, French and Italian, which in the end boiled down to the perennial dispute between the complex and 'artificial' on the one hand and the simple and 'natural' on the other.

The latter was championed by Rousseau (see page 46). Rousseau was an Italophile; but it must be remembered that he was supporting not Italian *opera seria*, which had made little if any headway in Paris, but *opera buffa*. It was the ingenuousness, simplicity and grace of such works as *La Serva Padrona*, *Il Maestro di Musica* (then also ascribed to Pergolesi) and Leonardo Leo's *I Viaggiatori* which seemed to Rousseau and his fellow philosophers, d'Alembert and Diderot, preferable to the stiff formality of Rameau.

One of the most influential of the Italian essayists was Francesco 66
Algarotti, whose *Essay on the Opera* (1755) was to have a profound influence on the thinking of Gluck. The suggestions he put forward for the improvement of Italian *opera seria* amounted to a return to first principles: music (instrumental and vocal), staging, decor, ballet, should be subservient to the drama, which should be chosen 'to delight the eyes and the ears, to rouse up and to affect the hearts of an audience, without the risk of sinning against reason or common sense'.

67 Niccolò Jommelli (1714–74). Before moving to Stuttgart he had built up a considerable reputation in Italy, with operas produced in Naples, Rome, Bologna and Venice. He had also been to Vienna, where he became friends with Metastasio. His last years were spent in Naples.

Unlike many of the French pamphleteers Algarotti was directly concerned with opera. He had been at Frederick the Great's court in the 1740s, translating opera libretti with the king; later he was at Parma, as artistic adviser in the ducal theatre there. This, administered on behalf of the Duke, Philip Bourbon, Infante of Spain, by a remarkably able Frenchman, Du Tillot, was at that time one of the leading European opera houses. The *maestro di cappella* from 1758 until Philip's death in 1765 was Tommaso Traetta, a composer almost completely forgotten today but important in the history of eighteenth-century opera. Gluck knew him and his compositions, among which we may note an *Ifigenia in Tauride* (1763) and an *Armide* (1760, in Vienna).

67 Another reform-minded Italian composer was Niccolò Jommelli, one of the Neapolitan school, who in 1753 became *maestro di capella* to Duke Charles Eugene of Württemberg, surviving in the service of that capricious old tyrant for fifteen years. Here he assembled a first-class orchestra (the famous violinist Nardini was its leader for several years) and some of the best singers of the time; there was a large and splendid *corps de ballet*, and the Duke spared no expense in mounting Jommelli's twenty operas. The German writer Schubart, who suffered a ten-year imprisonment at the whim of the Duke, has left an illuminating picture of the total control Jommelli exercised over his forces: 'He knew the singers, the orchestra, the audience, and through

68 Christoph Willibald von Gluck (1714–87), a somewhat idealized portrait by the fashionable Parisian artist Duplessis (1725–1802). Painted in 1775, it shows Gluck at the time of the Paris version of *Orpheus*.

the closest collaboration with the machinist, the stage designer and the *maître de ballet*, he could weld them all into one complete whole, so that he wrung the heart of the most phlegmatic hearer and carried him up to heaven' (quoted in Alan Yorke-Long, *Music at Court*). We seem to be looking forward more than a hundred years to Richard Wagner.

The *maître de ballet* in 1760 was the most distinguished dancer of his day, Jean-Georges Noverre, whose *Lettres sur la danse* (1760) was an outstanding contribution to the artistic debate. In it he protested against the meaningless acrobatics, the pointless gestures, the absurd costumes, that were degrading ballet, and instead called for an expressive simplicity, for mime. He had already dreamed of what was to be virtually a new art form, the dramatic ballet; he had been much struck by the potentialities of the form suggested by Rameau's operas, and had also been impressed by the acting of David Garrick, whom he had met in London. There can be no doubt that he exerted a direct influence on the thought of Count Durazzo, who from 1754 to 1764 was in charge of the imperial theatres in Vienna; on another Italian, also in Vienna, Ranieri Calzabigi; and on the composer whose name is most closely associated with eighteenth-century operatic 'reform', Christoph Willibald von Gluck (1714–87). *68*

Gluck, the earliest opera composer to retain a permanent place in the repertoire, though born in Germany was of Bohemian (that is, Czechoslovakian) descent, and passed his childhood and youth in

69 Gluck's opera, *Il Parnasso confuso*, performed in the Palace of Schönbrunn, Vienna, 1765. The cast was composed of members of the royal family (some of them, in costume, are in the front row of the audience). At the harpsichord is, possibly, Gluck himself.

Bohemia. He had about a dozen Italian operas performed in various centres in north Italy before he settled in Vienna in about 1747. There he set a few *opéras-comiques* to French texts (he never once wrote a German opera) before collaborating with Angiolini in a ballet, *Don*
70, 72 *Juan* (1761), and before the first of his 'reform' operas, *Orfeo ed Euridice* (1762), in Italian, with words by Calzabigi.

In this and the operas that follow, *Alceste*, words likewise by Calzabigi (Vienna, 1767), and the Paris operas, *Iphigénie en Aulide*
71 (1774), *Armide* (1777), *Iphigénie en Tauride* (1779) and *Echo et Narcisse* (1779), there is a deliberate return to the principles of music drama as expounded more than 150 years earlier by the Camerata, and explicitly formulated by Gluck in the famous Preface to *Alceste* –

principles which, as we have seen, had been adumbrated by Algarotti.

Gluck strove for a 'beautiful simplicity', and his methods are well illustrated in the first of these operas, *Orfeo ed Euridice*. This opens, not as in Monteverdi with the wedding festivities, but with Orfeo already mourning his loss in a dignified and controlled expression of grief. When, encouraged by Amor, he braves the nether regions, they are charmed, not as in Monteverdi by a richly ornate melody, but by an unassuming vocal line supported by uncomplicated harmonies on his lute (harp). Harmony as an emotional factor is apparent in the second act, but the powerful impression made by these choruses of lost spirits is equally referable to their homophonic nature. Though the overture is perfunctory, the orchestra elsewhere is given due weight and importance: Orfeo's 'Che puro ciel', a vision of the pure, golden radiance of Elysium, in sharp contrast to the previous Stygian gloom, is a classic example of tone-painting worthy to stand beside the best of Handel or Rameau, and was not without its effect on Gluck's musical successor and admirer Berlioz.

70 Design for *Orpheus* (Gluck), Act II, Entrance to the Underworld, by Adolphe Appia (1862–1928). Like much of Appia's work, this design was never realized in the theatre.

THOAS

Tunique de satin ponceau. manteau doublé de satin verd. Plumes d'un gris Roussâtre ; & d'autres noires.

71 (*left*) Costume design, by Jean Moreau ('le jeune'), for Thoas, in a production (1781) of Gluck's *Iphigénie en Tauride*. Costumes are beginning to move towards a more authentic style of dress (cf. *Ills* 105, 110).

72 (*above*) A modern design for Gluck's *Orpheus*, by Cesar Klein, for the Berlin State Opera (1927).

In the operas which Gluck wrote for Paris we see him single-mindedly pursuing these ideals. *Iphigénie en Aulide* is based on Racine, deriving ultimately from Euripides. Agamemnon and the Greeks are becalmed on the isle of Aulis, and to appease the goddess Diana a sacrifice is demanded – Iphigenia, Agamemnon's daughter. From this situation the expected moral dilemmas result. For Agamemnon it is the conflict between love for his daughter and defiance of the implacable goddess, with all that that might entail for the Greeks. Achilles, in love with Iphigenia, is eager to spring to her defence; but this would mean challenging Agamemnon, the father of his bride-to-be. For Iphigenia the choice is hard but clear; the decree is inevitable, and she must bow to it for the sake of her compatriots. The brooding overture sets the mood and leads without a break into the first scene. As in *Orfeo*, Gluck spurns vocal virtuosity, preferring to rely on directness and simplicity of utterance, backed by all the resources of harmony, orchestration and formal organization at his command.

French at this opera was in its avoidance of Italianate arias, its emphasis on the ballet and the importance attached to the chorus, in his next opera, *Armide*, he apparently set out deliberately to enter the field that was Paris's own speciality: the decorative opera. In fact, he chose to set the very text by Quinault that Lully had used nearly a hundred years earlier. It would perhaps be more correct to describe this romance of the Crusades, drawn from Torquato Tasso's *Gerusalemme liberata*, not as a 'decorative' but as a 'spectacle' opera, for Armida's magically transformed garden and the holocaust at the end, when her palace goes up in flames, bring to mind *Parsifal* and *Götterdämmerung*. For his last opera, *Iphigénie en Tauride*, his masterpiece, Gluck returned to Greek tragedy.

Gluck was a complex character, a blend of passionate sincerity and astute diplomacy, an idealist and a realist at one and the same time. He is the father of German opera; Mozart, Weber and especially Wagner stand indebted to him. In pre-revolutionary Paris his mantle fell not so much on Piccinni, who was inveigled into unwanted competition with him, as on two other Italians, his friend and pupil Antonio Salieri and Antonio Sacchini. Sacchini's *Dardanus* (1784), the full score of which was published in Paris in the same year, is a most interesting work; it is Gluckian in the use of the orchestra and in the cut of the music generally, but it also abounds in the sudden *sforzandi*, the nervous syncopations and the knitting together of sections by the use of motifs that are familiar to us in the music of Mozart. The same year also saw Salieri's *Les Danaïdes*, an equally impressive score. It was first advertised as by Gluck, and only after its success was its real authorship divulged. In his fine dramatic use of the orchestra Salieri is here at least the equal of Gluck, if not more; his vocal line, too, is supple and sensuous, and dramatically apt. Hypermestre, for instance, sings a pathetic arietta in G minor that can stand comparison with Pamina's 'Ach, ich fühl's' in *Die Zauberflöte*. For good measure, the final catastrophe adds an earthquake to the flames that destroy the palace.

## Comic Opera in the Eighteenth Century

Comedy poses some problems for the musician. In tragedy music is in its element; it and the drama can pull together. In comedy, or shall we say opera *non seria*, this is less easily achieved; indeed, if the comedy is verbal, or predominantly so, music may actually get in the way by making it more difficult for us to hear the words. This may be because the accompaniment is too loud, or too complex, and many composers are sinners in this respect. But the problem lies deeper than this, in that the voice in opera has a dual function. It relays both an emotional and a verbal message. The former demands a wide range of pitch; but this interferes with the clear enunciation of words. Some vowels are impossible to sing on a high note; consonants, which in at least some languages are vital to clarity of diction, are difficult to reconcile with beauty and continuity of vocal line. Then, too, the spoken word has a rhythm of its own; but the musical pace, dictated by the emotion or mood behind the words, may be either too fast or too slow for the verbal message to be easily intelligible to the audience. Also, song is slower than ordinary speech, but comedy often, if not always, demands speed; so one is tempted to work either at music's pace, in which case the comedy will drag, or, alternatively, at the appropriate speech pace, in which case the music is in danger of becoming a meaningless gabble. Add to this the differing requirements of low, men's voices as opposed to high sopranos, and the difficulties imposed by the auditorium itself, and it is evident why good comedies in music are rare.

One solution of the problem is to separate the emotional message from the verbal – to let ordinary speech carry the details of the intrigue, and bring in music as an emotional gloss and confine it to that. This is, broadly speaking, the principle of the French *opéra-comique*, the English comic opera, the German *Singspiel*, and carries over into operetta, musical comedy and the American 'musical'. It works well; but it disregards the possibility that music need not be restricted to this subordinate role but has a contribution of its own to bring to comedy. The discovery of how this could be done was one of the great achievements of the eighteenth century.

For the origins of this development we must turn again to Italy, and specifically to Naples, for it was there that *opera buffa* emerged early in the eighteenth century alongside the *intermezzo*. The *intermezzo* is in line with the *intermedi* which played their part in the early history of opera (see Chapter One), and as early as 1623, at Bologna, we find, inserted between the three acts of a serious opera, *L'Amorosa innocenza*, two *intermezzi* which form in fact a little two-act opera on its own. The device became popular; taking on a comic character, and played more or less farcically, with good comedians playing one or two stock characters with much 'ad-libbing' in the *commedia dell'arte* manner, it furnished light relief between the acts of a more serious work.

Who first fully grasped the significance of the new instrumental style which Durante, Pasquini and other composers were developing is immaterial. The short phrases, the nervous, staccato, rather disjointed type of melody, the rapid 'cross-talk' between voices, held together in a very clear system of tonality but with no pretence at a 'learned' technique, all added up to a musical language that was the perfect vehicle for comedy. Music began to develop a wit of its own; the petulant quirks of irascible old men, the pertness of insolent servants, could be etched in by abstract musical devices such as bustling, fussy bass lines, or by abrupt changes of register, or by the manipulation of the short tags or motifs which the instrumental composers were already using as their basic building materials. Repetitions of phrases, or of larger sections, were put to good use to help to clarify the action; for example, verbal points missed when they were first made would become obvious on a second hearing.

All these characteristics appear in fully developed form in
*74, 76* Pergolesi's *La Serva padrona* (1733), as fresh now as on the day it was written. There are three characters only: Uberto, Serpina his maid, and his manservant, who is mute and whose comedy is achieved entirely by mime. Serpina – young, coquettish, impudent – designs to become mistress of the household. Uberto, old and grumpy, puts up a show of resistance, but is foolish enough to imagine that Serpina has her eyes on him rather than his possessions. Much of the dialogue is written in the rapid *recitativo secco* of which the Italians alone seem to have the secret; but the real charm of the piece resides in the set numbers: the arias and duets. Here comedy and pathos are intermin-

73 A scene from the *commedia dell'arte*, showing Pantalone, accompanied by Arlecchino and two servants, serenading Donna Lucia. From a painting of *c.* 1580.

gled; we smile at Uberto, but are touched by his helplessness; Serpina may have a serpent's wiles (the name is a diminutive of *serpe*, 'snake'), but if she is a rogue, she is a lovable one.

This work, and the hundreds of *opere buffe* that followed during the next fifty years, have their roots in the old *commedia dell'arte*. Its *73*
tradition of extempore playing, topical gags, quick repartee and mime lay behind the comedies of Carlo Goldoni, Carlo Gozzi and a host of lesser writers from the libretti were adapted. The composers include Baldassare Galuppi, Francesco Feo, Leonardo Leo and Nicola Logroscino. Naples developed its own branch of the *opera buffa*, in its own dialect, and the last three of the composers just named were Neapolitans. Mostly forgotten today, their work was important in the development of ensembles, and in particular contributed to the

74 Giovanni Battista Pergolesi (1710–36).

75 Niccolò Piccinni (1728–1800).

evolution of the concerted finale that was to be such a notable feature of Mozart's comedies.

75 Two somewhat later Neapolitans were Niccolò Piccinni, the composer of one of the most widely played of all eighteenth-century *opere buffe*, *La buona Figliuola* ('The good Daughter'), to a libretto derived from Samuel Richardson's novel *Pamela*, and Domenico Cimarosa, whose best-known *opera buffa*, *Il Matrimonio segreto*, was written not for Naples but for Vienna. Another Italian to have had what is probably his *chef d'œuvre* produced outside Italy was Giovanni Paisiello, whose *Il Barbiere di Siviglia* was first heard as far from his native land as St Petersburg, in 1782.

The close ties noted in *opera seria* between Italy and the German-speaking lands also extended to *opera buffa*. Apart from the Italian composers already mentioned, whose works sooner or later found their way to Vienna, *opere buffe* were written by Austrians such as the Italian-trained Florian Gassmann and Karl Ditters von Dittersdorf, while the twenty operas which Joseph Haydn wrote for the Esterházys included a Goldoni libretto previously set by Galuppi, *Il Mondo della Luna* (1777). However, this wave of *opere buffe* sweeping up from the south was met by another strong current flowing from the north.

76, 77 Pergolesi's *La Serva padrona* ('The Maid as Mistress') in a production at La Scala, Milan, 1960–61; and (*below*) a sketch for the curtain, by Mario Pompei, for the production at La Scala, 1951–52, of *La Serva padrona* (1776), by Giovanni Paisiello (1740–1816).

78 While in the service of Count Esterházy Haydn wrote about twenty operas. The illustration shows a scene (set by Pietro Travaglio) from *L'Incontro improvviso* (1775), set to a libretto previously set by Gluck, performed in the theatre at Eszterház.

79, 80 (*right*) The old Burgtheater, Vienna. Built in 1741, it was transformed into a 'national' theatre (the Hof- und Nationaltheater) by the Emperor Joseph II. It was here that Mozart's *Abduction from the Seraglio*, *The Marriage of Figaro* and *Così fan tutte* were first performed.

The rising tide of *opera seria* had seeped into more and more centres during the course of the eighteenth century. The courtly preference for Italian music and Italian singers, forcibly expressed by Frederick the Great who scathingly compared German singing to the neighing of horses, was to endure into the nineteenth century, as Weber found to his cost. Even the famous old Goosemarket Theatre in Hamburg, which had worked valiantly for opera in German ever since it opened in 1678 with a biblical comedy, *Adam und Eva*, after fifty years was reduced to mounting an entirely Italian repertory (played by the Mingotti company, with which Gluck was later associated).

81 Nevertheless, though the courts of Vienna, Munich, Dresden, Berlin and Stuttgart (to name only the most important) indulged their tastes for the Italian style in music and decoration to the point of folly, the country was never completely submerged. As in Venice, the Hamburg Opera had no court to please, though it occasionally ran into trouble with the church; it never subscribed wholeheartedly to the Metastasian canon, and the operas of Reinhard Keiser (1674–1739) preserved the comic episodes of Roman and Venetian opera. This was
82 carried further by Georg Philipp Telemann (1681–1767), whose prodigious list of compositions includes a German counterpart of *La Serva padrona*, which in fact it antedates by eight years. Entitled *Pimpinone*, it has two characters only, Pimpinone and his maid, Vespetta, who wheedles him into marrying her. The score, which is available in a modern edition, shows that Telemann was as fully in command of the new *opera buffa* technique as his Italian contemporaries, Pergolesi and Leonardo Vinci.

81 Stage of the royal theatre, Dresden. Decor by Andrea Zucchi (1679–1740).

82 Georg Philipp Telemann, whose light, *galant*, up-to-date style was so much to the taste of his contemporaries that when the post of Cantor at St Thomas's church, Leipzig, fell vacant he was offered the post in preference to J. S. Bach. He wrote about forty operas, for Bayreuth, Eisenach and Hamburg.

The next phase of the *Singspiel* is somewhat complex, and a complete disentanglement of the threads would take us too deep, for present purposes, into German stage history. There were cross-currents from France (Frederick the Great was a confirmed francophile, while the operas of Grétry, Monsigny, Philidor and others had penetrated as far as Munich), and obvious connections between London and Hamburg and Brunswick. What was less predictable was that a ballad opera by a not particularly distinguished hack playwright, Charles Coffey, should prove one of the catalysts encouraging the precipitation of a distinctively German type of comedy with music.

This was *The Devil to Pay*, first produced at Drury Lane in 1731. A German version of this appeared a few years later at Berlin (1743); a new translation, *Der Teufel ist Los*, by Christian Felix Weisse, with music by Johann Christian Standfuss, was performed at Leipzig in 1752. The date, it will be noted, was that of the Italian performances in Paris that sparked off the 'Querelle des Bouffons' (see page 46). *83*

Standfuss's music was in an idiom that was to be characteristic of the *Singspiel* – unpretentious melody of a folk-like nature, harmonized in the simplest style, the kind of music, indeed, that was developing in Germany independently of the opera in the field of the solo song. It was further exploited and refined by later composers, notably Johann

83 The frontispiece to Charles Coffey's ballad opera, *The Devil to Pay*; or, *The Wives Metamorphosed*, published in 1731, showing three of the main characters: the doctor-cum-necromancer, who casts his spell on the two wives, the cobbler, and his wife.

Adam Hiller (1728–1804), whose connection with Leipzig shed a little lustre on that town's rather drab operatic history. It had possessed an opera house as early as 1693, but by the time Johann Sebastian Bach took up his duties at St Thomas's Church its opera had petered out. Bach's name is not popularly associated with opera, but it is noteworthy that in *The Peasant Cantata*, written in 1731, he sports a rustic style, incorporates folk-tunes, and generally gives us a foretaste of *Singspiel* a full twenty years before *Der Teufel ist Los*.

Between 1766 and 1777 Hiller wrote about a dozen *Singspiele*, all for Leipzig. For most of these his librettist was Weisse, who had a real flair for light and attractive verse, drawing on the French stage for most of his work. *Lottchen am Hofe* (1767) is a German version of the *Ninette à la Cour* set a decade earlier by Duni; *Die Jagd* (1770) goes back to *Le Roi et le Fermier*, with words by Sedaine, set by Monsigny in

84 Johann Wolfgang von Goethe (1749–1832) directed the Weimar theatre (*Ill.* 85 *below*) from 1791 to 1817. Besides *Singspiele*, some of which he wrote himself, he produced a number of plays, such as Schiller's *Don Carlos*, which subsequently provided material for operas. Weimar had a second period of theatrical importance in 1842–59, when Franz Liszt (1811–86) was musical director.

1762. *Lottchen* is a charming opera, a worthy forerunner of Mozart. Like Zerlina in *Don Giovanni*, Lottchen is dazzled by court life, but in the end comes to her senses and returns to her Gürge. Their music is simple and rustic, but, as befits a nobleman, that of Count Astolph is more elegantly wrought.

During the last quarter of the century the dominant influence behind the *Singspiel* remained that of the French *opéra-comique*, but parallel with this a fresh impetus was given to German opera by the dramatic activities of writers such as Wieland, Goethe and Schiller. *84*
Schiller's impact on opera was felt much later, in the nineteenth century (for example, in Rossini's *Guillaume Tell*, 1829; Verdi's *Don Carlos*, 1867), but Wieland and Goethe both contributed to the opera of their time. Wieland's *Oberon* was the source of Weber's masterpiece

of 1826, but he also wrote libretti for several contemporary 85 composers, while Goethe, whose work at Weimar was crucial for the whole German theatre, concerned himself with the *Singspiel* to the point of writing several examples (*Erwin und Elmire*; *Claudine von Villa Bella*; *Jery und Bately*).

This lively interest is reflected in the several attempts to establish a 'national' theatre. The *Alceste* of Wieland and Anton Schweitzer (Weimar, 1773) had been a conscious step towards a German national opera; it was followed a year or two later by an opera on a German, as opposed to a classical, subject, *Günther von Schwarzburg*, by Ignaz Holzbauer – called a *Singspiel*, but actually a full-blown opera, with recitatives (Mannheim, 1777). This, by one of the redoubtable group of Mannheim musicians, is a remarkable work in every way, with fully and richly scored recitatives, and with some vocal writing for soprano that rivals the Queen of Night's arias in *The Magic Flute* in range and difficulty. Mozart heard the opera and thought the music beautiful, and full of fire. In Vienna the first attempt at a 'national' opera was performed in 1778, as part of the Emperor Joseph II's praiseworthy attempt to foster the art of the theatre (he had founded 79, 80 the Burgtheater two years earlier). This was *Die Bergknappen* ('The Miners'), by Ignaz Umlauf – a *Singspiel*, followed over the next few years by several more examples by the same composer. These are now almost forgotten, but in 1782 the artistic seal was put on the *Singspiel* by the production, also in the Burgtheater, of Mozart's treatment of an already familiar theme, *Die Entführung aus dem Serail* ('The Abduction from the Seraglio').

In Vienna, the international crossroads of music, the simpler, northern, song-type *Singspiel* became fused with the softer, southern, Italianate, aria-orientated opera. Composers such as Gassmann and Dittersdorf, who had begun by writing *opere buffe*, turned now to the German-language *Singspiel*, but gave it a more sensuous, Italian flavour. Yet the time was not quite ripe. Mozart's next three operas were set to Italian texts, and other native composers such as Peter von Winter set Italian or German as the occasion demanded. Even Weber's *Der Freischütz*, perhaps the highest point attained by *Singspiel*, has a distinct vein of Italian music running through it.

# Mozart

Wolfgang Amadeus Mozart was born in Salzburg in 1756 and died in *89*
Vienna in 1791. This is only half a life; compared with Verdi or Wagner one might say that everything Mozart wrote was an early work. Yet it was he who, operatically speaking, crowned the eighteenth century, and he is the one composer from this period whose works remain abundantly alive, with no need whatsoever for indulgence or special pleading.

This in the first place is because musically he dwarfs all the others. We hardly need Handel's famous remark, that Gluck knew no more of counterpoint than his cook, to convince us of Gluck's lack of it; it stares us in the face in every score he wrote. Mozart, on the other hand, moved in the realm of polyphony with the ease of Bach, and often with more grace; and what is more, he could put it to dramatic use. Likewise, his command of harmony was second to none, and again almost every page of his dramatic works provides object lessons in the use of this resource to support the action. He not only had the older techniques of recitative, aria and so on at his fingertips, but was fully in control of, and saw clearly the dramatic relevance of, the newer sonata-form principle – a technique which the older Gluck never mastered, and perhaps never attempted to master. And finally, his touch with the orchestra was unsurpassed, with instrumental colour linked in the most felicitous manner to the happenings on the stage.

To this immense musical competence Mozart brought a dramatic intelligence of the highest order. It must be remembered that in his time both the straight drama and the lyric stage were approaching a turning point. In the older drama, for example, it had never been thought necessary to justify logically every entrance and exit. Shakespeare brings his characters on and sends them off quite freely; they come, make a point, then 'exeunt', followed by others. Nor in *opera seria* did anyone bother to ask just why two characters should find themselves at a particular corner of the palace, with a third character, accidentally there at the same time, eavesdropping. If

86, 87 Cherubino discovered hidden in an armchair in the Countess's chamber; a scene from Beaumarchais' (1732–99) play, *Le mariage de Figaro*, 1784. *Below:* a design by Joseph Platzer for the garden scene in the last act of Mozart's *The Marriage of Figaro*; the first Prague performance, 1786.

88, 89 Aloysia Lange, *née* Weber. Mozart fell in love with her, but actually married her sister, Constanze. Aloysia sang Donna Anna in the 1788 Vienna production of *Don Giovanni*. *Right:* Wolfgang Amadeus Mozart (1756–91).

librettists had been challenged, their reply could have been a simple one: in real life we *do* meet people by chance, and think nothing of it. But comedy, with real-life characters instead of two-dimensional symbols from the realms of classical mythology or ancient Roman history, demands a tighter and more highly organized framework, and no doubt part of the attraction for Mozart of Beaumarchais's *Le* *86*
*Mariage de Figaro* was precisely the ingenuity and logic of it.

Moreover, the exact ordering of the entries and exits often contributes materially to the dramatic total. In the second act of *Le Nozze di Figaro* ('The Marriage of Figaro'), for instance, the Count, *87, 90, 93*
baffled by a locked door behind which he suspects the Countess has hidden a lover, exits, to seek tools to break open the door. He has a good reason for his exit, and an equally good one for returning. The audience's grasp of the situation is heightened by the knowledge that he *will* return; their enjoyment of the scene is enhanced far more by this logical certainty than it would have been by any chance encounter. The whole of the complicated finale that follows is packed with such nicely calculated points, as when the gardener bursts in in a temper to complain that a man has been thrown out of the window on

90 Nancy Storace (1766–1817), an English singer, the first Susanna in *The Marriage of Figaro*. 91 Elisabeth Schwarzkopf as Donna Elvira in *Don Giovanni*. 92 Henriette Sontag (1806–54), one of the most accomplished coloratura sopranos of her day, notable as Susanna and as Donna Anna in *Don Giovanni*. She was also the first Euryanthe in Weber's opera of that name (see *page* 140). 93 Elisabeth Schumann (1885–1952) as Countess Almaviva in *The Marriage of Figaro*. 94 Mary Paton (1802–64), a Scottish singer and a great stage beauty, and another outstanding Susanna.

95 Don Giovanni is claimed by the powers of hell. Louis Otey as Giovanni in the 1983 production by Mark Lamos for the Opera Theatre of St Louis, conducted by Christopher Hogwood.

to his flowerbed (it is in fact Cherubino, who has jumped out of the window to escape the Count).

This tautness of construction explains why *Figaro*, for all the complications of its plot, is so supremely satisfying. It is so neat that we are hardly aware of the complexity. There are very few loose ends. *Don Giovanni*, the second of the operas written in collaboration with *91, 95*
Lorenzo da Ponte, is less tidy; nevertheless, our appreciation of the last act depends a good deal on the hint that, at some time during the supper scene, the marble statue of the Commendatore is (probably; we know he accepted the invitation) going to join the Don and Leporello.

In *Così fan tutte*, the third of the Da Ponte operas, the handling of *96, 97*
exits and entrances is not quite so trim. The main idea is excellent; the six characters – the two pairs of lovers, the cynical old bachelor, the accommodating maid – are the very stuff of artificial comedy, and

96 (*left*) A portion of Mozart's autograph score of *Così fan tutte*: the beginning of Guglielmo's aria, 'Donne mie la fate a tanti', from Act II.

97 (*below, left*) Walter Berry, Anneliese Rothenberger and Rosalind Elias, in *Così fan tutte*, Salzburg Festival, 1969.

98 (*right*) Lorenzo da Ponte (1749–1838).

their characterization is superb. But the details of the departure of Guglielmo and Ferrando and of their return as their real selves are less convincing. The conjuring up of a complete regiment for them to join, and a ship in which they embark, wafts us out of the everyday world, which is the region of comedy, into the realm of fantasy. Despite some of the most ravishing music Mozart ever wrote, *Così* was virtually ignored in the nineteenth century, when the plot was thought to be immoral. Today it is played as frequently as the other two comedies.

Lorenzo da Ponte (1749–1838), one of those raffish, colourful 98
characters that enliven the history of the eighteenth-century theatre, deserves at least a short paragraph to himself in any history of opera. He took minor orders in the priesthood, but found this not incompatible with the fleshly pleasures of eighteenth-century society. After being brought up in Italy he went to Vienna as court poet to Joseph II, writing libretti not only for Mozart but for other composers such as Martini and Salieri; Martini's *Una Cosa rara*, an aria from which is quoted in the last act of Mozart's *Don Giovanni*, was set to a libretto by him. After this he lived for a time in London, doing hackwork for the theatres there; he then emigrated to America, where he taught Italian at Columbia University. He also had a hand in establishing Italian opera in New York. With no great original talent as a poet, he had a lively pen; his *Memoirs*, written late in life in

America, have been compared to those of Casanova.

For the forerunners of Mozart's animated and highly sophisticated art we have to look not to *opera seria*, which was too constrained and formal (in both a good and a bad sense), but to two separate but interlocking developments. The first was *opera buffa*. Taking many of its ideas and some of its characters from the vast reservoir of the *commedia dell'arte*, it differed in spirit from the pastoral-sentimental style of French *opéra-comique* and from its German derivative, the bucolic *Singspiel*. It was faster moving, with characters who were sharper-witted; its situations were nearer to those of real life. There is virtually no equivalent in *opera buffa* of the French Rose or Lubin, whose dalliance in their rustic Arcadias moves at an almost aristocratically leisured pace; Hans and Lisel live in a well-ordered Teutonic feudal society, where everyone knows his place. Their more nimble Italian counterparts inhabit a far less stable world, but a world nearer to reality.

In *La Serva padrona* Serpina's outspokenness is possible because she is separated from her foolish old master not by class, but by the mere accident of possessions; Figaro and Susanna, on the other hand, are pert rather than impertinent, and however revolutionary Mozart's opera may be in some respects it makes no real attempt to bridge the gap between them and their superiors, the Count and the Countess. It does, however, move with a pace that would leave the characters of eighteenth-century *opéra-comique* and *Singspiel* gasping.

The second factor was the increasing preoccupation with the orchestra and the symphonic forms, which were emerging as compact structures with their own purely instrumental logic. Orchestral accompaniments, built from insignificant straps of melody fitted together to make coherent tonal schemes, became self-sufficient; nevertheless, they supported and illumined the stage action. Opportunities naturally increased as orchestras grew in size. The chattering oboes would often wittily underline the garrulity of the 'patter' arias; the easy tone of the flute added its own touch of tenderness to a soprano solo, while the 'buffo' baritone (tenors were too precious, too 'singing-orientated' to lend themselves readily to comic business) found himself echoed by the cello or the bassoon.

The more purely musical devices that were the supports of the larger symphonic structures were also seen to have their dramatic uses. A strong determination not to be put upon was underlined in the

99 Anton Raaff (1714–97), German tenor, who created the title role in Mozart's *Idomeneo*, Munich, 1781. By this time his voice had begun to deteriorate, and, according to Mozart, he was not a good actor. But Mozart liked him, and, as he wrote to his father, did his best 'to show some courtesy to his grey hairs' by writing music that he could manage to sing.

orchestra by the emphatic perfect cadence; the interrupted cadence could express astonishment, consternation. Choice of key had always been important – D major for military pomp, G minor for pathos, D minor for the typical 'rage' aria, and so on. Now, with the weakening and final abandonment of the unity-of-mood doctrine – the principle that each aria should be restricted to one sentiment only – key contrast assumed greater importance. A new mood, a fresh factor in the web of intrigue, came to be signalized by a dramatic change of key; doubt, indecision, the self-searching in soliloquy form, expressed in the accompanied recitative by such tonally ambiguous chords as the diminished seventh, could now be further intensified by restless modulatory passages driving us disturbingly far from the main key centre.

These are symphonic devices, and opera drew nourishment from their use in sonata, symphony and above all the concerto. The 'concertante' style, with two, three or more soloists played off against the rest of the orchestra, is a situation paralleled over and over again in operatic ensembles, especially those of Mozart. It is no accident that it

100 Set by Giovanni Carlo Bibiena (d. 1760), for an earlier (1755) *Clemenza di Tito*.

was Mozart, whose handling of the ensemble may have been equalled but has never been surpassed, who raised the concerto to its most exalted height; his last five great operas teem with echoes of the masterly concertos written between 1782 and 1786, seemingly as substitutes for the operatic contracts which were so disappointingly slow to come his way.

In all, Mozart composed twenty-two stage works of various kinds, including several that remain unfinished. Ten, including the delightful *Bastien und Bastienne*, were written in his teens. His first big opportunity came when he was asked to write an *opera seria* for
*99, 101* Munich, in 1781. This was *Idomeneo, Re di Creta*, and here, in his first mature opera, he handles his materials with an almost ostentatious flourish of musicality. Virtuosity is harnessed to artistic ends not merely through the singers (the arias as a matter of fact are not exorbitantly taxing) and the orchestra, but also by means of such musical factors as modulation, form and harmonic resource. Com-

101 A simple but poetic set by John Napier for Trevor Nunn's 1983 Glyndebourne production of *Idomeneo*. Carol Vaness (Elettra), Philip Langridge (Idomeneo), Jerry Hadley (Idamante) and Margaret Marshall (Ilia).

pared with this achievement, Gluck's technique looks amateurish. Eric Blom writes of *Idomeneo*: 'It is the great *opera seria* of a composer not peculiarly fitted for that species.' In fact, *opera seria* was dying; Mozart's last work in that vein, *La Clemenza di Tito*, written for the coronation of the Emperor Leopold II in Prague in 1791, showed that even he, at the height of his powers, could not altogether resuscitate it.

We remember Mozart today for his comic operas. Some of the drawbacks of grafting music on to comedy have been noted at the beginning of Chapter Six, but there are compensatory advantages. In the spoken theatre the actor holds our undivided attention, but in opera this is shared with the orchestra. This may support the singer by adding its own tremulous sighs or fluttering heartbeats (in a letter to his father Mozart instances one such example in *The Abduction from the Seraglio*), or it can slyly give the lie to the singer's protestations. It can enrich the stage action in a thousand different ways.

Above all, there is the ensemble, which offers a means of

102 Design by Giuseppe Quaglio (1747–1828) for the production of *The Magic Flute* in Munich in 1793.

103 The first act of *The Magic Flute*: Tamino, Papageno and the Three Ladies – and the Serpent, well and truly dead.

simultaneous presentation quite denied to the 'straight' theatre, where more than one person speaking at once leads only to confusion. But in opera this is the composer's great opportunity, limited only by his own command of counterpoint and his librettist's skill with words. The ensemble was not Mozart's invention but was evolved largely by forgotten Neapolitan composers of comic operas, not to mention Handel, whose pastoral *Acis and Galatea*, which Mozart may have come across in London and which he 'arranged' later in his life, contains some delicious examples of music speaking with two minds.

Mozart's great comic masterpieces begin with *Die Entführung aus dem Serail* (1782) – to give it its proper title, since it is technically a German *Singspiel*; though in spirit the music looks across the border to Italy. The plot, a favourite one, derives ultimately from England, but the main characters, especially the comic servant, Osmin (one of the great bass roles), and Selim Pasha, the amorous despot, hankering for the pretty imprisoned Constanze, are derived from the Italian *opera buffa*. In so far as the hero, Belmonte, plots to abduct Constanze from the harem, the plot leans towards the later 'rescue' opera, while Selim's magnanimity at the end and the concluding vaudeville link it to the stately Metastasio type and French *opéra-comique*.

His next German opera, *Der Schauspieldirektor* (1786), was a slight affair, but the situation – two rival *coloratura* sopranos besieging the luckless impresario – furnished rare opportunities for characterization and parody. His last German opera, *Die Zauberflöte* ('The Magic *102–104*
Flute', 1791), has been described as 'the apotheosis of the *Singspiel*'. It was commissioned by Emanuel Schikaneder, the manager of the small Viennese Theater auf der Wieden. He also wrote the book, which he designed as a 'magic' opera, a species then having a considerable vogue in Vienna, and he took care that it should have a rewarding comic part for himself – Papageno. The resulting combination of ritual, magic and symbolism, interspersed with circus-like clowning which borders on the farcical, made a powerful appeal to Mozart's nature, which was a compound of all these things. With this opera Mozart scored at last a great popular success, but later nineteenth-century audiences found it difficult to classify or accept and dismissed it as having a feeble plot which could not be rescued even by Mozart's enchantment. They disapproved of their serious musical pleasures being adulterated by pantomime. But audiences are now losing some of their prejudices against mixed genres, and today *The Magic Flute*, with its presentation

104 David Hockney's design for *The Magic Flute* at Glyndebourne (1978); production by John Cox. Thomas Thomaschke as Sarastro, Willard White as The Speaker.

on two levels, the spirituality of the Tamino-Pamina duo set off against the earthy Papageno-Papagena relationship, its half-revealed Masonic mysteries, its conflict between good and evil, perhaps even the ambivalent quality of the Sarastro-Queen of Night relationship, is seen as a quasi-religious work which inspires in some quarters an almost mystic veneration.

With the three Da Ponte Italian operas, *The Marriage of Figaro*, *Don Giovanni* and *Così fan tutte*, we at once reach the apogee of *opera buffa* and say farewell to it. It lingered on a little while, in Cimarosa (whose best work, *Il Matrimonio segreto*, appeared in the year after Mozart's death), in Paisiello and in Rossini, whose *The Barber of Seville* (1816) had to fight hard against Paisiello's 1782 version. But with Rossini we turn over a new page; the French Revolution had swept away *opera seria* and *buffa*, *Singspiel* and *opéra-comique* into a forgotten land.

CHAPTER EIGHT

# Post-Revolution Opera in France, Italy and Germany

During the last few years of the *ancien régime* the Paris Opéra pursued its course with admirable equanimity, seemingly unaware of the coming storm. It had had to move to new quarters in 1781, when the premises in the Palais Royal were burnt out. A 'provisional' theatre in Boulevard Saint-Martin was run up in the short space of three months; like so many temporary buildings this outlived its intended life, to be in its turn destroyed by fire nearly a hundred years later, in 1871. There the classical tradition was maintained by the Italians, now well entrenched in the wake of Gluck. Piccinni was represented by *Didon* (1783), *Diane et Endymion* (1784) and *Pénélope* (1785). Sacchini's *105*
*Dardanus* and Salieri's *Les Danaïdes* have already been noted; the latter was followed in 1786 by *Les Horaces* and in the following year by a notable collaboration with Beaumarchais, *Tarare*. Cherubini, who arrived in Paris via London, where one or two of his operas had been given with little success, had his first Parisian opera, *Démophon*, performed in 1788, but his most impressive operas were post- *108*
Revolution. All these works were performed in French.

Native composers (Grétry, Gossec, Dalayrac, Philidor) followed in general the lines laid down by Lully and Rameau; their musical style was little if at all different from that of the repertoire at the Opéra-Comique (in the Salle Favart since 1783). Grétry's *Richard Cœur de Lion* (1784) and Dalayrac's *Nina ou La Folle par Amour* (1786) might be cited as typical. They were *opéras-comiques* rather than *opere buffe*, with spoken dialogue interspersed with airs and the smaller *ariettes*, and very little ensemble.

During the period of the Revolution and the Directory, the artistic standing of the Paris Opéra was nil, with only a sorry parade of revolutionary sycophancy. In 1792, for instance, was performed '*L'Offrande à la Liberté, scène religieuse sur le Chant des Marseillais.* Musique de Gossec (Rouget de Lisle, Dalayrac)'. In 1793 Gossec, now Citoyen Gossec, gives us *Le Triomphe de la République ou le Camp de Grandpré*, a *divertissement* in one act. Later, in June, we have *Le Siège de*

105 The move towards authenticity in costume, and away from ostentation for its own sake: Moreau's costume for Dido, in Piccinni's *Didon*, Paris, 1783 (cf. *Ills* 86, 110).

106 (*right*) To the Parisian citizen of 1789 the Opéra, under the protection of the court, was the symbol of privilege, and on 12 July – two days before the fall of the Bastille – a hostile crowd demonstrated before the building, effectively closing the Opéra. The last performance attended by the royal party (Rameau's *Castor and Pollux*) was in 1791.

*Thionville*, lyrical drama, by Citizen Jadin, and in October *Fête pour l'Inauguration des Bustes de Marat et de la Peletier*, performed in the street in front of the Opéra, with music by Gluck, Gossec and Philidor. Once Napoleon became Emperor, due homage had to be rendered with such pieces as *Chant du victoire en l'honneur de Napoléon; orné de divertissements guerriers*, given on 9 November 1806. It was indeed not until he had been on the throne for three years that a major new production was performed at the Opéra – Spontini's *La Vestale*, in 1807.

The less formal Opéra-Comique fared better, and during the last decade of the eighteenth century mounted a number of operas that opened a new chapter in operatic history from the point of view of choice of themes, if not as yet in their treatment. In 1790 Grétry joined forces with a young writer, Bouilly, to produce *Pierre le Grand*, in which, as in Lortzing's later *Zar und Zimmermann*, the hero is the young Peter the Great of Russia. In 1791 Grétry followed this up with

a treatment of the Swiss revolutionary, *Guillaume Tell*, thus anticipating by some years not only Rossini (1829) but Schiller (1804). Then in 1793 a younger compatriot, Jean François Lesueur (1760–1837), broke new ground with *La Caverne*, based on an episode from Le Sage's *Gil Blas*. It is a 'brigand' opera, the forerunner of many, including Auber's *Fra Diavolo* (1830), and also Hérold's *Zampa* (1831), which is a better opera than the rather brash overture might lead one to suppose.

Two other composers who deserve some mention are Etienne Méhul (1763–1817) and Henri Montan Berton (1767–1844). Méhul's twenty-five operas range from Ariosto (*Ariodante*, 1798) to Ossian (*Uthal*, 1806). For his best work, *Joseph* (1807), he went to the Bible – a *107*
source that has always seemed congenial to French composers, for example Montéclair (*Jephté*, 1732), Saint-Saëns (*Samson et Dalila*, 1877) and Milhaud (*David*, 1954). Berton's forty or so operas include a very popular 'rescue' opera, *Les Rigueurs du Cloître* (1790), wherein we encounter many of the ingredients that became overworked in the

107 Giuseppe Quaglio's sets for the 1809 Munich production of *Joseph*, by Etienne Méhul (1763–1817), were an early attempt to bring verisimilitude and local colour into the performance of opera.

romantic operas of the first decades of the nineteenth century – assignations with a young novice in a convent, the uncovering of damaging secrets, a trial scene, impressive *religioso* scenes inside the convent, and a final last-minute rescue by a troop of soldiers. The score is by no means lacking in interest; there are already the passages of nervous figuration, the little groups of repeated notes on the main beat of the bar, the syncopations, that were to be prominent fingerprints of the Italian music of the next generation.

In the following year, 1791, Cherubini consolidated his growing reputation with another 'rescue' opera. This was *Lodoïska*, a highly coloured melodrama set in Poland, on the Russian border. It ends with quite a Wagnerian holocaust: the castle in which *Lodoïska* has been incarcerated by the nefarious Doulinsky is bombarded and collapses in flames, but *Lodoïska*, needless to say, is rescued from it by her lover Floreski. The music, especially the finales, is built up in broad sweeps, with much power and imagination. At that time Cherubini could

108 Cherubini's *Médée*, originally produced in Paris in 1797, lay largely forgotten until revived at the Florence Maggio Musicale in 1953. Maria Callas is seen here in the title role.

109 Costume design by Comelli for the 1893 London production of *La Juive*, by Halévy (1799–1862).

110 Fernand Cortez, the Spanish leader, in the Paris production of Spontini's *Fernand Cortez*. First performed in 1809, it was revised and mounted again in 1817.

hardly have known the big Mozart works of the 1780s, but he had no doubt studied the Salieri operas already published in Paris. At the first performance the decor won special praise; the first act ('Forest; a Castle, with a Tower; trees, rocks') shows the preoccupation with sublimity in nature that was beginning to dominate painting. In another of his operas, *Elisa* (1794), the action takes place in the Alps, with an avalanche thrown in for good measure.

Two other 'rescue' operas are of particular interest by reason of their relationship with the classic 'rescue' opera, Beethoven's *Fidelio* (1805). They are Cherubini's *Les Deux Journées* ('The Water Carrier', 1800), a work immensely admired by Beethoven, and the slightly earlier *Léonore, ou l'Amour conjugal*, by Pierre Gaveaux (1798). The

111 The Temple of the Gods, in Spontini's *Fernand Cortez*, designed by Lorenzo Sachetti (1759–*c.* 1836) for the 1825 Berlin performance.

libretti of both were by Bouilly. The first is set in Paris in the time of Cardinal Mazarin; for the second, which was substantially to supply the plot for Beethoven's opera, Bouilly drew on a supposed incident in the French Revolution but transferred the scene to Spain, in some indeterminate period. This theme, of the wife or lover faithful unto death, returns also in Halévy's best work, *La Juive* (1835). *109*

All these works were given at the Théâtre Feydeau (the Opéra-Comique); the artistic resurrection of the Opéra, now christened the Académie Impériale de Musique, dates really from 1807 and was due to Gaspare Spontini (1774–1851). Although he wrote twenty-nine operas in all, his reputation rests in the main on three works, all written for Paris – *La Vestale* (1807), *Fernand Cortez* (1809) and *Olympie* *110, 111*

112 Philippe de Loutherbourg (1740–1812), a painter from Alsace, was also a theatrical designer. This striking picture and others like it gave a lead towards the more 'romantic' treatment of scenery in the theatre.

113, 114 *Right:* The last scene of *Undine*, by E.T.A. Hoffmann (1776–1822), design by Karl Friedrich Schinkel (1781–1841) for the 1816 Berlin production; and set by Alessandro Sanquirico (1777–1849), the foremost Italian scenographer of the time, for the Milan production of Giovanni Pacini's (1796–1867) *L'Ultimo giorno di Pompeia.*

(1819). Cast in the grand, rather statuesque mould that has been a continuing characteristic of French serious opera ever since the days of Lully and Rameau, they set new standards in the opera house, with their rich scoring (Berlioz considered Spontini, with Weber and Beethoven, one of the contemporary masters of the art), sumptuous decor and careful attention to detail. Spontini raised orchestral playing to new heights, both in Paris and Berlin, whither he moved in 1820; he and his contemporaries Louis Spohr and Weber were the first generation of great interpreters in the opera house. Like Weber and Wagner, he supervised every detail of the productions, to the immense gain of the work as a whole. In *Fernand Cortez*, for example (the theme had been suggested by Napoleon, who seems to have

imagined that an opera on the conquest of Mexico would somehow reconcile the French people to the Spanish campaign), we have for the first time an attempt at treating an historical subject realistically. No expense was spared in mounting the work; it was a 'spectacular', not the least of the attractions being a cavalry charge. But the sets were constructed with some attention to topographical credibility, and exceptional pains were taken over the costumes to distinguish between uniforms of the Spaniards and the dress of the Mexican warriors.

Nevertheless, Spontini was an anachronism. His choice of subjects, his librettists, his style of music, were relics of the eighteenth century, and when he left Paris his supremacy was already being challenged by an active group of younger composers busy laying the foundations of the new-style 'romantic' opera. These composers included Adrien Boieldieu, Daniel François Esprit Auber, Ferdinand Hérold, Fromental Halévy and Adolphe Adam (best-known for his ballet *Giselle*). For their material they rejected the mythological subject in favour of the new plots, new situations, new heroes, to be found in the younger writers of melodrama such as Mélesville, Delavigne and Scribe, as well as in the more enduring dramas of Victor Hugo.

Examining the music of these composers, one becomes aware of a new tone of voice. Something of the detachment and dignity of the classical eighteenth century has gone, replaced by a more impassioned utterance; the restraint of reported incidents has yielded to the depiction of violent action on stage. For the expression of this in music a new language was needed, the inspiration for which came from Italy, and by the mid-nineteenth century opera nearly everywhere again meant Italian opera.

In Italy, and to some extent in Germany, the watershed between the *ancien régime* and the new look in politics and art was less the French Revolution than the Napoleonic wars and their aftermath. It is this fact that goes some way to explain the peculiar position of Gioacchino
*117* Rossini (1792–1868). Though seemingly up to date, his musical idiom remained in fact basically an expansion of eighteenth-century *opera seria* or *opera buffa* techniques. Building on the foundations laid by such men as Sarti, Cimarosa, Paisiello, Zingarelli and Generali, he added to a natural tunefulness a piquancy of orchestration and a resourcefulness of melodic decoration which caught the ear of the public wherever his operas were played. And how the public

115 Rossini's *The Barber of Seville* at La Scala, Milan, 1964–65. Production by Franco Enriquez, sets by Giulio Coltellacci.

responded! Few composers can have been so fêted as Rossini; his catchy tunes, exhilarating rhythms, the verve of his famous crescendos, the sheer animal spirits of his music swept Europe off its feet.

The formula proved of most lasting value in the realm of *opera buffa* (*L'Italiana in Algeri*, 1813; *Il Barbiere di Siviglia*, 1816). His serious *115*
operas (*Tancredi*, 1813; *Otello*, 1816; *Mosè in Egitto*, 1818; *Maometto II*, 1820; *Semiramide*, 1823) fell into neglect in the first half of this century. More recently they, and others, have been successfully revived and recorded.

He was in the van of the 'historical' opera, especially of those derived from the romances of Sir Walter Scott. *Elisabetta, Regina d'Inghilterra* (1815), based on *Kenilworth*, followed a few years later by *La Donna del Lago* ('The Lady of the Lake', 1819), set a fashion for the *116*
British Isles that was taken up enthusiastically by Boieldieu (*La Dame blanche*, 1825) and Donizetti (*Lucia di Lammermoor*, 1835; *Alfredo il Grande*, 1823; *Anna Bolena*, 1830) among others.

116 Rossini's *La Donna del Lago*, at Covent Garden, London, in 1847; an artist's impression, in *The Illustrated London News*.

Rossini's connection with the French stage had always had happy results. One of his most engaging comedies, *La Cenerentola* (1817), was a working of the Cinderella story, already used by Isouard and Steibelt, taken from the seventeenth-century writer of fairy stories, Charles Perrault; *The Thieving Magpie* (1817), a *semiseria*, was based on a very successful French play, *La Pie voleuse*, which in Italian translation as *La Gazza ladra* was also a great favourite on Italian stages. From about 1825 he made Paris his headquarters, and during his period as Director of the Théâtre Italien he did much to foster Italian opera and the *bel canto* style of singing. While there he wrote his
118 last comedy, the vivacious *Comte Ory* (1828), and then in his masterpiece, *Guillaume Tell* (1829), he finally joined some of his juniors in the historico-political arena.

Only the year before, the Opéra had staged Auber's *La Muette de*

117 The youthful Rossini; portrait, by an unknown artist, in the Liceo musicale, Bologna.

118 Set by Jean-Pierre Ponnelle for the 1957 Berlin production of Rossini's *Le Comte Ory*, clearly inspired by the well-known fifteenth-century illuminated manuscript, *Les très riches heures de Jean Duc de Berry*, now preserved at Chantilly.

*Portici*, the story of the Neapolitan fisherman, Masaniello, who led the 1648 revolt against the Spaniards. It was very likely the success of this that tipped the scales in favour of *Tell*, a 'revolutionary' opera still banned in the Papal States in the 1840s. Rossini worked long and lovingly over this intricate score, and one can scarcely doubt that its comparative lack of success confirmed him in his resolve to write no more for the stage. It was his last opera, even though he was to live nearly forty more years.

Various reasons have been put forward in explanation of his self-imposed silence. He certainly suffered from ill health, and gallstones can be abominably painful. But ill health can be overcome, if the will is there; and it was not. He may well have been reluctant to compete with the younger musicians working in a new idiom which was uncongenial to him, though he had helped to create it. Brilliant and effective though his music is, it is lacking in human warmth; it glitters rather than glows. The intimate and melting sweetness of Mozart and the powerful sweep of Verdian melody are rarely in evidence. The nearest approach to the latter's impassioned musical speech is to be found in *Tell*, in, for example, Arnold's 'Ah! Mathilde, idole de mon âme' from Act I, or Mathilde's 'Pour notre amour' from Act III.

The ardent, unselfconscious outpouring that issued so reluctantly from Rossini came with sincerity and total conviction from the Sicilian Vincenzo Bellini (1801–35), in whose music we hear for the *120*
first time the unmistakable nineteenth-century Italian accent. As a student in Naples he came under Rossini's spell, but already his first opera, *Adelson e Salvini*, written while he was still at the Conservatoire, reveals his own individuality. Like many of his contemporaries (Chopin and Liszt come to mind), he regarded virtuosity as a legitimate means of expression, the vocal elaboration in, for example, Amina's music in *La Sonnambula* (1831) or Norma's miraculous 'Casta Diva' emerging as the natural and apparently spontaneous outcome of the emotional or dramatic situation. Where the need arises he can be touchingly simple, and his thrusting, vibrant melodies are often invested with an extraordinary urgency and power. In his love music we find a new tenderness and rapture; the thrilling ecstasy in his Romeo and Juliet opera, *I Capuleti e i Montecchi* (1830), was the prototype of the impassioned outbursts of Verdi and Puccini.

His greatest works were written in collaboration with the most gifted Italian librettist of the day, Felice Romani, who wrote altogether more than ninety opera books. Romani continually turned to France for his material, and *Il Pirata* (1827), *La Sonnambula* and *Norma* (1831) were all, like Verdi's *Rigoletto* and Puccini's *Tosca*, based on Parisian stage successes. There was even an abortive *Ernani*, based on Victor Hugo, but this got no further than a few sketches, for in 1830 it stood little chance of passing the Italian censor and was withdrawn, the harmless *Sonnambula* being substituted.

Bellini lived and worked in an Italy divided against itself and under foreign domination. Overt radical acts or opinions were dangerous, but three of his operas – *Bianca e Fernando*, *Norma* and *Beatrice di Tenda* – have political implications. The third (the last he wrote to Romani's words, in 1833) was probably the first Italian opera to attempt a serious presentation of Italian history (it is set in the fifteenth century, with Philip Visconti as the central character), while in *Norma* the parallel between the plight of ancient Gaul in Roman times and modern Italy under the Austrian yoke was obvious.

119 Gaetano Donizetti, painted in April 1848, not long before his death, by the Bergamo painter Rillosi.

120 Vincenzo Bellini; a portrait by an anonymous artist, painted in 1825 or thereabouts.

121 Giuditta Pasta (1798–1865) was outstanding in such dramatic and forceful roles as Medea and Norma. She was a soprano with a big voice, of wide compass, and her lower notes were exceptionally powerful, though, as a vocalist, she was less technically accomplished than some of her rivals.

His operas have tended to be associated in people's minds with brilliant, 'coloratura' sopranos of the calibre of Maria Callas or Joan Sutherland, but they are far more than just vehicles for this type of voice and in fact need not one fine singer but a team of fine singers. His was an era of magnificent performers, and the list of those associated with him during his lifetime is a golden roll of honour. Tosi, Méric-
*121* Lalande, Pasta, Giulia and Giuditta Grisi, Malibran, Caroline Ungher,
*123* Caradori-Allan, Lablache, Tamburini, David, Bonfigli, Reina, Donzelli, Rubini – in the whole history of opera it would be difficult to overtop such a star-studded galaxy. Moreover, from all contemporary accounts, their acting was, at its best, on a par with their singing. Pasta, the Grisi sisters, the mercurial Malibran, may perhaps have overplayed their parts, at least according to present-day notions; but this was an era when tragic actors and actresses were expected to be larger than life. It was the age of Edmund Kean, and of the Kemble family, at least one of whom scored a success on the operatic stage. 'Mad' scenes were popular; Elvira's ravings in *I Puritani*, the sleep-walking scene in *La Sonnambula*, Norma's agonized indecision over the killing of her two sons, and Imogen's long-drawn-out, crazed
*122* agony in the last act of *Il Pirata*, all offered opportunities for the exaggerated mime expected by every audience as a matter of course.

Bellini being a true Italian, the voice has pride of place, but his orchestration is by no means without its touches of genius, as for instance in the last scene of *Norma*. His big polaccas, as in *Bianco e Fernando*, *I Capuleti* and *I Puritani*, and his impressive finales show a capacity for large-scale organization, while in *La Straniera* in particular he seemed to be working towards a new approach, with less emphasis on coloratura and an increased attention to thematic unity and harmonic richness. He was a more forward-looking composer than is often supposed, and his early death was a severe blow to Italian opera.

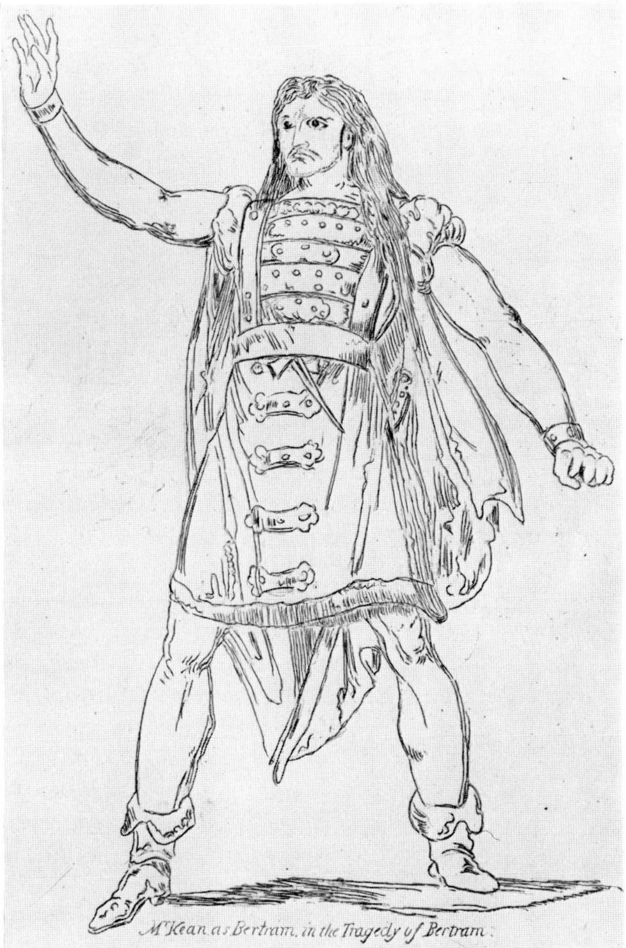

Mr Kean as Bertram, in the Tragedy of Bertram.


122 Bellini's opera *Il Pirata* (1827) was based on a popular and highly melodramatic tragedy, *Bertram*, by the Irish writer Charles Robert Maturin, the basis of the Paris play from which Romani took his libretto. *Bertram* was first produced in London in 1816, with Edmund Kean (1787–1833) playing the title role (Gualtiero in Bellini's opera).

123 Luigi Lablache (1794–1858), half Irish, half French, but brought up in Italy, one of the finest operatic singers of all time. His voice was a rich bass, and he played with success both serious and comic parts. He is seen here as the quack doctor, Dr Dulcamara, in Donizetti's *L'Elisir d'Amore*.

Bellini's chief rival (to his suspicious nature any other composer was
119 an enemy) was Gaetano Donizetti (1797–1848). Compared with Bellini, for whom composition was a slow and painful process, Donizetti was versatile and if anything too facile. Much of his time as a young man was frittered away on ephemeral farces, and it was not until 1830 that he proved his mettle in *Anna Bolena*, written for Pasta and produced at the Teatro Carcano, Milan. His long list of over seventy operas includes three comedies – a genre which Bellini did not
123 attempt. *L'Elisir d'Amore* (1832), *La Fille du régiment* (1840) and *Don Pasquale* (1843) have kept a continuous hold on the public, as have *Lucia di Lammermoor*, *Lucrezia Borgia* and *La Favorite*, at least when there have been sopranos able to sing them. The story of his last years makes sad reading; shortly after *Don Pasquale* his mind began to give way, and he was confined for a time in an asylum before being taken back to his native Bergamo, where he died.

124 Jenny Lind (1820–87), one of the finest sopranos of the nineteenth century. Though she sang all dramatic roles, such as Norma, she was perhaps at her best with less powerful characters, such as Amina in Bellini's *La Sonnambula*, or, as here, as Marie in Donizetti's *The Daughter of the Regiment*.

125, 126, 127 (*left*) Three of the world's most illustrious opera houses. The oldest of the three is La Scala, Milan (*top*), built in 1778. Severely damaged in 1943, it was rebuilt and reopened in 1946, much as it was. At Naples there was an opera house adjacent to the palace in 1737, but the present San Carlo (*centre*) dates from 1816. The Vienna State Opera (*below*) was opened in 1869. Totally destroyed during an air raid in 1945, it was rebuilt, and reopened in its former splendour in 1955.

128 Playbill announcing the first performance of Beethoven's *Fidelio*, 1805.

Turning to nineteenth-century Germany and Austria, one is immediately struck by the small contribution made to opera by the great composers (discounting Wagner). Brahms and Bruckner wrote none at all, and Mahler confined himself to completing an unfinished comedy by Weber (*Die Drei Pintos*, 1888). Mendelssohn toyed with it; Schumann left one interesting experiment (*Genoveva*, 1850). Schubert, much more enthusiastic, left at least seventeen operas in various stages of completeness, but few were performed in his lifetime other than his substantial incidental music to the play *Rosamunde* (1823). Beethoven wrote one opera and Weber completed six, but the bulk of German operatic literature was supplied by composers of the second rank, such as Spohr, Marschner, Lortzing, Nicolai and Goetz.

Beethoven's *Fidelio* was first produced in Vienna in 1805, with *128, 129*

129 Ludwig van Beethoven (1770–1827); a portrait, in oils, by the Viennese artist Ferdinand Georg Waldmüller.

130 (*right*) Charles Edward Horn (1786–1849) as Caspar, in Weber's *Der Freischütz*, at the Drury Lane theatre, London, 1824.

indifferent success, and a revision in the following year did comparatively little to improve matters. Yet another recasting took place in 1814, and this is the version now usually performed. It is a 'rescue' opera; but it is far more than that. It is an ode to nobility of soul and the dignity of man. It is the second great German opera, *Die Zauberflöte* being the first; both are in the *Singspiel* form but both transcend its limitations. But while *Die Zauberflöte* adheres to the older convention, which equates ordeals and sacrifice with noble birth, Florestan's courage and Leonora's steadfastness are qualities that shine through them simply as human beings.

Weber's approach to opera was fundamentally different. Far more of a literary man than Beethoven, he was much influenced by the writers of the day, many of whom he counted among his friends. They were the standard-bearers of the new German Romanticism, a movement that was essentially mystical and spiritual, as distinct from the rationalism of the eighteenth century and the new humanism, if it may be called such, inspired by the French Revolution. They turned to the legendary past or the chivalric Middle Ages for sustenance – an attitude which reached its operatic climax with Wagner. But it was a field already being tilled by Weber, notably in *Euryanthe* (1823), and also by Schumann in *Genoveva* – two works whose musical idiom was already moving significantly in the direction of the language needed by Wagner for his music dramas.

*130* Weber's masterpiece is *Der Freischütz* (1821), and it is interesting to compare this, the first great German romantic opera, with the earlier *Fidelio*. Virtue triumphs in both; but while in *Fidelio* it is Leonora's personal fortitude that foils the wickedness of Pizarro, in *Der Freischütz* the victory becomes more abstract; it is the force of goodness that eventually overcomes the spirit of evil. Max indeed is no hero, and Agathe's role is a passive one. Moreover, while there is no hint of the supernatural in the humanist *Fidelio*, the crux of *Der Freischütz* is the Satanism in the Wolf's Glen scene, depicted with full romantic and musical force, its diabolical F sharp minor music ultimately routed by the beatific C major with which the opera begins and ends.

Weber's last opera, *Oberon*, set to a libretto based on Wieland's poem, was performed at Covent Garden theatre in April 1826, a few weeks before the composer died in London. It remained the most recent opera to have been commissioned by Covent Garden from a non-British composer until Henze's *We Come to the River* was premiered there exactly 150 years later.

# Late Nineteenth-century Opera in Italy and France

The man who epitomizes Italian nineteenth-century opera is Giuseppe Verdi (1813–1901). Since he was born in the same year as *137* Wagner, and since these two are unquestionably the dominant figures in nineteenth-century opera, their names inevitably tend to be coupled. In fact they have hardly anything in common. True to his country's tradition Verdi preferred the natural to the supernatural; he had little sympathy with mysticism, mythology or magic; recondite symbolism or abstractions such as 'redemption through love' had no appeal for him. Instead he preferred to work with the all-too-human qualities of ambition, greed, envy, love, jealousy, loyalty, heroism. His own nature was uncompromising, upright and sincere; but he could be prickly, rough and ungracious. His characters express themselves with a directness that reflects his own forthrightness, and in his choice of subjects his leanings were to simple, strong, melodramatic situations that well repaid such treatment.

131 Verdi's birthplace, in the little village of Le Roncole, near Busseto, some twenty-five miles north-west of Parma.

132 Pauline Viardot Garcia (1821–1910), the younger sister of Maria Malibran (1808–36), very unlike her sister in temperament but an equally great artist. She is seen here as Azucena, in Verdi's *Il Trovatore*.

133 Marcella Sembrich (1858–1935) as Violetta in Verdi's *La Traviata*.

Melodrama was indeed woven into his early life. In 1814 a party of Russian soldiers, busy weeding out any remaining French sympathies
*131* from Napoleon's toppled empire, looted the little village of Le Roncole where Verdi was born. Women and children sheltering in the church were massacred, but Giuseppe and his mother escaped; she had hidden in the campanile. His early years were a struggle against poverty; as he later put it simply to a friend: 'My youth was hard.' He obtained his first professional appointment at the age of twelve (as organist at Le Roncole, on a pittance), while in near-by Busseto his practical musical education continued through contact with small-town music-making (wind band and orchestra).

134 A scene from Franco Zeffirelli's production of Verdi's *Aida*, at La Scala, Milan, 1962–63.

A malignant fate pursued him even into manhood. In 1836 Verdi had married Margherita Barezzi, the daughter of his first benefactor (the courtship had been conducted via piano duets). By her he had two children, a boy and a girl. Neither lived much more than a year. Then, in June 1840, his young wife died. Verdi's own account, oddly enough, telescopes these searing experiences into the space of three months; the real time-scale is sufficiently shattering, and he was left crushed and distraught. If ever a man was tempered in the fire of adversity it was Verdi.

Throughout this period of black despair he was sustained and
*136* encouraged by Bartolomeo Merelli, the impresario at La Scala theatre, Milan, who had given him his first contract. It was Merelli who coaxed him back to composition; the result was *Nabucco* (1842), which quickly brought wider recognition. *Nabucco*, the first opera to carry his name outside Italy (it reached Paris in 1845 and London, where there were objections to its biblical subject, the following year), had a topicality which the Milanese recognized; it had also a new force

135 The second scene of Act II of Verdi's *La Traviata*; an artist's impression of the 1856 London production at Her Majesty's Theatre, London.

136 The impresario Bartolomeo Merelli (1794–1879).

137 Giuseppe Verdi.

and power which both public and critics acclaimed. It was, as one writer observed, 'agitators' music'; and the same note can be detected in three other works that quickly followed: *I Lombardi* (1843), *Ernani* (1844) and *Luisa Miller* (1850).

The political flavour is, if anything, intensified in the revolutionary hymn of 1848, *Suona la tromba*, and in the opera *La Battaglia di Legnano* of 1849, but vanishes utterly from the three masterpieces of the early 1850s: *Rigoletto*, *La Traviata* and *Il Trovatore*. This apparent retraction *132, 133, 135* must be seen against the background of the disastrous reverses suffered by the over-optimistic insurgents in 1849. Verdi's letters of the time tell of his despair and disillusionment at the turn events had taken. After the defeats in Rome, Venetia, Piedmont and Lombardy, the Austrians seemed so securely in the saddle that Verdi would have had to be exceptionally clairvoyant to see the tables turned ten years later, and himself from 1860 to 1865 a Member of the Chamber of Deputies of the new Kingdom of Italy.

In *Rigoletto* and *La Traviata* Verdi had been lucky enough to hit upon well-constructed plays (Victor Hugo's *Le Roi s'amuse* and

Alexandre Dumas' *La Dame aux Camélias*), but he was not by any
means always so fortunate. He had no literary pretensions and never
attempted to write his own libretti, though he badgered his librettists
increasingly as he grew older. Unlike Wagner he had no theories, only
his instinct, to guide him; and his instinct sometimes let him down.
The plots of *Simon Boccanegra*, *La Forza del Destino*, *Un Ballo in*
138 *Maschera* and *Don Carlos* are all open to criticism on the grounds of
complexity or improbability, or both. Yet Verdi accepted them
readily enough, finding compensation in the scope which they offered
for strong characterization and powerful situations. On the other
139 hand *Les Vêpres siciliennes* (1855), commissioned by the Paris Opéra,
was not at all to his liking. Eugène Scribe, the librettist, had already
written one opera book concerning a massacre (Meyerbeer's *Les
Huguenots*), and no doubt saw this remote thirteenth-century story of
Italian treachery and French incompetence simply as 'good theatre',
with situations that ought to appeal to Verdi. But to Verdi it smacked
of insincerity, and he composed it with reluctance.

142 Sometimes, as with *Un Ballo in Maschera* ('A Masked Ball'), the
censor intervened, with ludicrous results. The libretto was based on
that originally prepared by Scribe for Auber, dealing with the

138 A design for *Don Carlos*, by Carlo Ferrario, the scenographer whose work Verdi is said to have preferred.

139 Operatic subjects not infrequently appear as material for pictures. Francesco Hayez, a Milanese artist in Verdi's circle, executed several paintings on Verdian themes, including an *I Due Foscari* and at least two dealing with the Sicilian Vespers. One of the latter is illustrated here; it dates from 1845.

assassination of Gustav III, King of Sweden (the original motive for the assassination had been purely political, but Scribe injected a love motive). The Italian censorship was almost as touchy as the Russian where royalty was concerned, but the transference of the locale to colonial Boston, Mass., did nothing to assist the opera's credibility. Nowadays it is usually performed in the Swedish setting.

Throughout these operas there is a noticeable widening and deepening of Verdi's purely musical resources. Whereas previously he had laid on his colours with a broad brush, he now paid greater attention to detail, with subtler shading and better characterization; the orchestra, which he had always handled boldly (there is some marvellous wind writing in the early operas) is used with an increasing finesse. These half-dozen or so operas that followed *Il Trovatore* represent a sort of second apprenticeship, the prelude to the three towering masterpieces of his last creative period.

140 Teresa Stolz (1836–1902), a great Verdi singer (she sang Aida in the first La Scala performance of the opera) and a close friend of both Verdi and his second wife, Giuseppina Strepponi.

141 (*right*) Cover of the original edition of *Aida*, based on a stage setting for the 1872 Milan production of the opera.

*134, 141* The circumstances surrounding the composition of *Aida* were for some time swathed in picturesque legend. It was written neither for the opening of the Suez Canal, nor for that of the Cairo Opera House; it was, however, commissioned by the Khedive of Egypt in 1870 and after many difficulties and delays the first performance eventually took place in the new Cairo house on 24 December 1871. The story combined all the qualities dearest to Verdi's heart – love, patriotism, devotion, steadfastness and courage – and he reacted to it with the warmest and most satisfying score that he had yet written. To his unique capacity for direct and heartfelt melody were added a new intimacy, a fresh appreciation of orchestral colouring and a bolder counterpoint. In grandeur of conception and magnificence of staging it surpassed *A Masked Ball* and *Don Carlos*; it fused soloists, chorus, orchestra, ballet, decor and lighting into a triumphant sublimation, a rich amalgam of French grand opera with Italian music drama.

It was, he thought, his swansong. He was now prosperous, and in the prime of life (he was fifty-eight), but his energies turned more and more to his cows and his vines on his farm at Sant'Agata, and he viewed the prospect of the immense labour involved in large-scale composition with increasing reluctance.

AIDA
DI
VERDI
EDIZIONI RICORDI
PROPRIETÀ PER TUTTI I PAESI - DEPOSTO A NORMA DEI TRATTATI - DIRITTO DI TRADUZIONE RISERVATO

142 Marian Anderson made history as the first black singer at the Metropolitan, New York, in 1955 in the part of Ulrica in Verdi's *A Masked Ball*.

Some of Verdi's problems as an opera composer lay with his librettists; at long last, in Arrigo Boito, he met a partner worthy of him. Boito was a younger man, a poet and a composer; his *Mefistofele*, to his own libretto, produced in 1868, remains one of the best Faust operas. It took a good deal of artful cunning to get Verdi to his writing desk again, but Giuseppina Strepponi, his second wife, and Giulio Ricordi, the head of the Milan music publishing firm, did it between *143, 144* them. The results were *Otello* (1887) and *Falstaff* (1893). Boito's libretti are among the best ever written; we can go further and say that between them Boito and Verdi produced not only the two finest of all Shakespeare operas but the supreme achievements of all Italian opera.

Verdi's practical, commonsense approach to theatre-craft left little room for attitudinizing or moralizing. Though fully conscious of his own powers, he disclaimed any suggestion of infallibility and totally abjured any doctrine of a composer's 'divine right'; for him the public was the arbiter, its judgment final. He preached no message, but his tragedies, by the intensity and integrity he brought to them, have a spiritual value, and effect a catharsis, sometimes denied to works by more pretentious composers.

143 The French singer Victor Maurel (1848–1923) as Falstaff, the role which he created at La Scala in 1893.

144 The Italian tenor Giovanni Martinelli, a fine interpreter of the title role in Verdi's *Otello*.

145 Design for Meyerbeer's *Le Prophète*, Act III, Scene 4, by some member or members of the Grieve family, who were important scenic designers in London during the first half of the nineteenth century.

146 Set for Meyerbeer's *Robert the Devil*, by Pierre-Luc-Charles Ciceri (1782–1868), who was the principal designer for the Paris Opéra during the first half of the nineteenth century.

It is this lack which, for all their earnestness of purpose, we sense in the works of the man who dominated the French stage for so long, Giacomo Meyerbeer (1791–1864). His real name was Jakob Beer, and he was born in Berlin. He was one of Weber's circle. He had had a few operas produced in Germany and Italy before he arrived in Paris in 1826, but his reputation rests on those he wrote in collaboration with Scribe for the Opéra – *Robert le Diable* (1831), *Les Huguenots* (1836), *Le* 146, 171
*Prophète* (1849) and *L'Africaine* (produced in 1865 shortly after his 145
death). *Robert the Devil* is a fantastic, melodramatic blend of the supernatural and the horrible, in the vein popularized by M. G. Lewis's novel, *The Monk*, but the others drew on the fashionable 'historical' subject; *The Huguenots*, for instance, exploits the St Bartholomew Massacre of 1572, and *The Prophet* deals with another religious theme, the Anabaptist rising in Holland in the sixteenth century.

These monumental stage spectacles – French 'grand opera' *par excellence* – were accepted throughout the nineteenth century as the *ne plus ultra* of operatic entertainment, the counterpart in their day of the 'colossal' film epic of our own. Every detail was meticulously supervised by Meyerbeer; the sets, by Ciceri, were lavish and naturalistic – a style that continued in the work of succeeding scenographers such as Jambon and Jusseaume.

Of the French composers of the time the greatest but the least appreciated was Berlioz, only one of whose complete operas appeared in France during his lifetime. This was *Benvenuto Cellini*, produced at the Opéra in 1838. Berlioz's lofty ideals of what the theatre should be were not those of Second Empire Paris, which would have found his masterpiece, *Les Troyens*, static and untheatrical. His attempts to have it staged (described in graphic detail in his *Memoirs*), even after he had sacrificed the unity of his conception and adapted it in two parts, were unavailing, though he did succeed in having the first two acts performed as *La Prise de Troie* ('The Capture of Troy') in 1863. Even when, in 1890, both parts (*La Prise de Troie* and *Les Troyens à Carthage*) were at last staged, the opera suffered cuts and other mutilations, and in fact the first complete performance of the work, as Berlioz had conceived it, did not take place until 1969, when it was mounted both by Scottish Opera and at Covent Garden. *Les Troyens* was long (so 147
were Meyerbeer's popular successes) and made no concessions to either the theatrical or musical fashions of the day, but it is brimful of

147 A scene from Scottish Opera's 1969 production of Berlioz's *The Trojans*, with Janet Baker singing Dido.

Berlioz's own especial genius, and for those who have been privileged to see it it remains a cherished dramatic experience.

If Berlioz is *sui generis*, an individual not easily classifiable, yet his Frenchness is unmistakable; and this applies equally to another group of composers. In Ambroise Thomas, born in 1811, and Charles Gounod, born in 1818, the Italian mannerisms found in Auber, Boieldieu and Hérold have all but completely vanished. Their music, tuneful, graceful, unadventurous harmonically and lightly scored, has a French *chic* all its own; it inaugurated what was virtually a new genre of opera, although like operetta (with which it has many affinities) it is a continuation of the eighteenth-century French tradition. Gounod
148 was perhaps the most robust of the two. His *Faust* (1890) must be one of the most successful and widely played operas ever written; others

148 The Polish bass Edouard De Reszke (1853–1917) as Méphistophélès in Gounod's (1818–93) *Faust*.

149, 150 Lucienne Bréval (1869–1935) in the part of Salammbô (Ernest Reyer, 1823–1909) which she created in 1901; and Lily Pons as Lakmé in Delibes' opera. It was this role that launched her in 1928.

that contain admirable music are *Le Médicin malgré Lui* (1858), *Romeo et Juliette* (1867) and *Mireille* (1864). The line was continued by Jules Massenet (1842–1912) – whose twenty-seven operas include *Manon*
150 (1884) and *Werther* (1892) – and Léo Delibes (1836–91), whose *Lakmé* (1883) is among the best of those operas which exploited the then fashionable exoticism of far-Eastern subjects.

Georges Bizet, who died in 1875 at the age of thirty-six, is in a different category. Working in the same milieu but with an incomparably wider range of melody, harmony and orchestral colour, he showed a far greater gift of characterization in such works as *Les Pêcheurs de Perles*, *Djamileh*, *La Jolie Fille de Perth*, and the masterly incidental music to Daudet's *L'Arlésienne*. His last opera,
152 *Carmen* (1875), still technically an *opéra-comique* by reason of its spoken dialogue, not only surpasses all his own earlier works but outclasses all others in its field. From one point of view it is the first and greatest of

151, 152 Leontyne Price as Thaïs, in the production of Massenet's opera given in 1959 by the Lyric Opera of Chicago; and Madame Nuovina as Carmen, Paris, 1898.

the *verismo* operas (*verismo* being the word coined to denote works focusing on the seamier side of life such as the later Mascagni, Leoncavallo and Puccini revelled in), and as such it was incomprehensible to the patrons of the Opéra-Comique, who felt that the respectability of this state-subsidized theatre had been sullied by what one critic described as 'Castilian licentiousness'. Bizet's crime in *Carmen* was that he refused to have the story prettified, its savagery and cruelty diluted, and in this he was backed up to the hilt by the first Carmen, Galli-Marié, who startled the audience by the realism and abandon of her interpretation. It is curious, by the way, to read that the orchestra found some of the music unplayable, and that the chorus grumbled that theirs was unsingable. How far we have come in a hundred years!

153, 154 Bust of Charles Garnier (1835–98), the architect of the Paris Opéra. Begun in 1861, the colossal and overpoweringly ornate building (*below*) was at long last, *avec la plus grande solennité*, and in the presence, among others, of the Lord Mayor of London, inaugurated on 5 January 1875.

# Wagner and Music Drama

Richard Wagner (1813–83) was born in Leipzig, the stepson (possibly *155*
the son; there are still doubts as to his paternity) of an actor. His family was far from affluent, but he was given a fair education, at schools in Dresden and Leipzig. The theatre was his ambition, and while still in his teens he wrote a grand tragedy, *Leubald*. So far he had had no thought of becoming a composer, but on hearing some Beethoven he suddenly realized that his tragedy needed music. He grappled with the problem of composition with characteristic energy, largely on his own, and with such success that he had an overture performed when he was only seventeen. His first compositions were all instrumental, and included piano sonatas and a symphony.

His first practical contact with opera came when he was about twenty, when he was engaged as *répétiteur* to a second-rate company in Würzburg which gallantly struggled with a mixed French, Italian and German repertory. While there he wrote his first opera, *Die Feen* ('The Fairies'), based on a short story by Gozzi and not staged until after his death. Whether it can be said that his next opera, *Das Liebesverbot* ('The Ban on Love', based on Shakespeare's *Measure for Measure*), really had a performance or not is a moot point. It was the final *débâcle* in a disastrous season at Magdeburg, whither Wagner had moved after Würzburg. The first night was a shambles, with the singers quite unable to sustain their parts, and the orchestra at sixes and sevens; on the next night, which was to have been the composer's benefit, a fisticuff bout between the leading lady's husband and her lover developed into a free-for-all backstage, and any hope of a performance had to be abandoned.

Wagner next went to Riga, where he stayed for about two years and wrote his third opera, *Rienzi*, based on Bulwer Lytton's novel of the same name. Composed with an eye to the Paris Opéra, it was on the same colossal scale as *William Tell* or *The Huguenots*, and ended with a fine holocaust, the Roman Capitol in flames. It eventually (1842) received a good production under Wagner, not in Paris but in

155 Richard Wagner, one of the very few men of whom it can be said that he changed the course of music history.

*156, 157* Dresden, with a cast that included Wilhelmine Schröder-Devrient and Tichatschek.

*Rienzi* was the last work of what might be called his years of apprenticeship, when he was endeavouring to establish a foothold with either Italian- or French-style conventional opera. In his next three works he moved away from this naturalistic region into the misty lands of legend and myth. The theme of *Der fliegende Holländer*, the Dutch sea captain condemned to sail the seas for ever for his rash defiance of the Devil, was already gestating during Wagner's time at Riga; his flight from his creditors in that city (a cloak-and-dagger adventure story in itself) involved a storm-tossed and hazardous three weeks' sea voyage to London which made an indelible impression on his mind and stamped *The Flying Dutchman* with its unique character. The menacing, cruel sea runs through this opera as it does through Benjamin Britten's *Peter Grimes*.

Wagner's objective was Paris, where he arrived in 1839; but his two-and-a-half years there brought nothing but bitter disillusion. The story of how he eked out a miserable existence arranging French operas and operettas for piano, or for cornet solo, is well known. But it was in Paris that he began the study of the rich store of German medieval poetry which became the basis of all his later work. The first
*157* results were *Tannhäuser* (1845), produced in Dresden, where he
*158* became *Kapellmeister* in 1843, and *Lohengrin*. This had also been

156, 157, 158 Wilhelmine Schröder-Devrient (1804–60, *right*) and Joseph Tichatschek (1807–86, *below left*) were two of the early singers who believed in Wagner, and on whose work Wagner could rely. They both created roles in two of his early works, *Rienzi* and *Tannhäuser*. *Below right:* The Czech tenor Leo Slezak (1873–1946), a favourite of the Viennese public, seen as Lohengrin.

159 King Ludwig II of Bavaria (1845–86). His father, Maximilian, had laboured to make Munich an artistic and literary centre, and when Ludwig became king in 1864 he continued the patronage but channelled it towards the musical stage. It was through his efforts that *Tristan und Isolde* (1865), *Die Meistersinger von Nürnberg* (1868), *Das Rheingold* (1869) and *Die Walküre* (1870) were all given first performances at Munich, before the new theatre at Bayreuth was built.

intended for Dresden, but Wagner's political activities in 1848 and 1849 had cost him his job; a warrant was out for his arrest, and once more he had to flee. He joined the ranks of political exiles, and did not set foot in Germany again until 1861. Meanwhile Liszt, who was to become one of Wagner's most ardent champions, produced *Lohengrin* in 1850 in the small theatre at Weimar.

The years of exile in Switzerland were given over to didactic writings such as *The Artwork of the Future* (1850) and *Opera and Drama* (1851) and to the labours preparatory to his later works, particularly *Der Ring des Nibelungen*. The evolution of this monumental work, which over a period of years grew from a *Siegfrieds Tod* (intended in the first instance for Liszt's small forces at Weimar) to the huge tetralogy that it finally became, was in itself a saga of almost superhuman effort, worthy of its titanic subject.

During the 1860s Wagner's fortunes began to change. In 1861 he at last reached the Paris Opéra, with a performance of *Tannhäuser* celebrated in operatic history for a disorderliness rivalled only by the

first night of Stravinsky's *Rite of Spring* in 1913. His earlier works were
gradually becoming more widely known (*Tannhäuser*, for example,
the first Wagner opera to be heard outside Europe, had reached New
York in 1859); then in 1864 began the association with the young,
idealistic King Ludwig II of Bavaria, whose munificent patronage *159*
made possible the crowning of Wagner's life's work. *Tristan und
Isolde*, the first new Wagner opera since *Lohengrin*, was first heard at *164*
Munich in 1865. *Die Meistersinger von Nürnberg*, originally conceived
by Wagner as a lightweight comedy, was given in Munich in 1868.
Munich also witnessed the appearance, in 1869, of *Rheingold*, the first
of the four operas which form *The Ring of the Nibelung* ('Festival Play *165*
for Three Days, with a Preliminary Evening'). The second, *Die
Walküre* ('The Valkyrie') was presented at Munich in 1870; the third *166*
and fourth, *Siegfried* and *Götterdämmerung* ('The Twilight of the *167*
Gods'), were first given as part of the first performance of the
complete cycle at the specially built Festspielhaus (Festival Playhouse) *160–62*
at Bayreuth in 1876. Wagner's last opera, *Parsifal*, appeared at *168*
Bayreuth in 1882.

These later operas are without rivals for size, complexity and grandeur of conception. The libretti were his own, and whatever their value as literature the labour involved in their preparation was immense. They exist in one or more drafts, beginning with a detailed scenario in prose; the poetic versions, in a linguistic style based on the techniques of German medieval poetry, cost him endless trouble. They were the fruit, too, of an exhaustive preliminary study of all the sources he could lay his hands on. Musically his problems were just as formidable. He was the heir to a long instrumental-cum-symphonic tradition which culminated in Beethoven's great range of symphonies, of which he was an outstanding interpreter. He saw this tradition as something essentially and fundamentally German, and set himself the task of incorporating it into a multiform 'artwork of the future' – a synthesis of poetry, drama, music, decor and lighting – which would produce a theatrical experience of a quasi-religious kind. Like others of his time, for example Ibsen, he conceived of the theatre not as a mere means of entertainment but as something ennobling and spiritually uplifting, after the ancient Greek example. It was to this end that he designed his ideal theatre, the Festspielhaus at Bayreuth, a temple of art where his sublime conceptions could be enjoyed in conditions as near perfect as possible.

160 The exterior of the Festspielhaus, Bayreuth, 1876.

The stage was Wagner's pulpit, from which he preached sermons in
*165–67* sounds. *The Ring* is a vast morality play, extolling the virtues of heroism and fortitude, condemning cupidity and falsehood. The idyllic innocence of the Rhinemaidens in their watery paradise is shattered by Alberich's lust for power, but the gold that he wrests from the river's depths becomes tainted by his very act, and even the gods are not immune from its baleful influence. Their destruction paves the way for a new dispensation, a regenerated mankind freed from the contemptible vices of greed, envy and malice. There is much else in *The Ring*; Robert Donington's *Wagner's 'Ring' and its Symbols* delves deeply into the inner significance that modern depth psychology reads into these archetypal myths.

As with most moralists, Wagner's vision stopped short of piercing the veil of the New Jerusalem, though perhaps through Hans Sachs,

161, 162, 163 The simple design of the auditorium in the Festspielhaus (*top*), in marked contrast to the richly ornate interior of Bibiena's old Bayreuth theatre (see *Ill.* 65). Each seat afforded a good view of the stage. On the stage is Max Brückner's 1882 set for the Temple of the Holy Grail in *Parsifal* (the first performance), seen in more detail in the centre picture. It is interesting to compare this heavily decorated set, which Wagner liked, with Wieland Wagner's austere design (*below*) – the outcome of the theories of Adolphe Appia (see *page* 170).

164 The Swedish soprano Birgit Nilsson, as Isolde in *Tristan und Isolde*; she was one of the post-war period's outstanding interpreters of this most exacting role.

165, 166, 167 *Above:* Behind the scenes in the 1876 production of *Das Rheingold* at Bayreuth; the Rhinemaidens are seen 'swimming', cradled on supports based on trolleys that are trundled about the stage. *Right:* Kirsten Flagstad (1895–1962) in one of her most magnificent roles, that of Brünnhilde in *Die Walküre*. *Below:* Though Appia's ideas were slow to penetrate Germany, some contemporary designers in other countries were moving in the same direction. This is a set for *Siegfried*, Act III, by the French scenographer Amable (1902).

168 The great Wagner roles have been interpreted by singers of many nationalities. Milka Ternina (1863–1941), a Yugoslav, is seen here as Kundry in *Parsifal*.

the cobbler-poet hero of *Die Meistersinger*, we may learn, by his wisdom and moderation, how to reconcile man's spiritual and practical needs, how to live as an individual in a community, how to look with forbearance on the frailties and follies of mankind.

It must be noted that Wagner was not working in isolation. The material he used, namely the Nibelungen sagas and other legends, was common property. As early as 1840 Mendelssohn had gingerly toyed with the idea of a Nibelungen opera; this came to naught, but an opera on the subject was actually realized by Heinrich Dorn in 1854 (when Wagner's was only at the libretto stage). The year 1840 had seen the performance of a Meistersinger opera, *Hans Sachs*, by Lortzing. On the 'legitimate' stage there appeared in 1858 a *Brünhild*, by the poet
169 Emmanuel Geibel, and four years later a trilogy, *Die Nibelungen* (which Wagner did not think much of), by the composer's exact contemporary Friedrich Hebbel.

But though Wagner conceived his music dramas as a fusion of the arts, there is no question that it is the music above all else that engages our attention, and it is this that distinguishes them from the operas of his contemporaries. Wagner's works seem to owe little to any previous operatic practice; the stage action, instead of being, as it were, supported, in aria and recitative, on a more or less solid musical base, is suspended in a fluid tonal continuum that recalls the majestic flow of Bach in his Passions and cantatas. The voice declaims in a supple, chromatic and wide-ranging line, half recitative, half *arioso*, and strictly syllabic. The formal aria has gone completely; so too has the substructure of sections, sharply differentiated from each other in mood, pace and key, that had been so valuable a listener's guide in the past. The vastly extended time-scale is ordered by an intricate lattice of 'leading motifs' (*Leitmotiven*), descriptive or suggestive, rhythmic, melodic, harmonic and often richly chromatic, regulating both the dramatic and the musical structure. They lie mostly in the orchestral tissue, but when they do erupt into the vocal line, as when we hear the 'Siegfried' motif in the full glory of Wotan's vocal splendour at the end of *Die Walküre*, the effect can be overwhelming.

The essential paradox of Wagner is that for all his preoccupation with the drama and reverence for Gluck it is the music which in the end is all-important. The inexorable flow of the Rhine, the fire spurting from the rock and encircling Brünnhilde, the consuming passion of Tristan and Isolde, the solemnity of the Pilgrims' March in *Tannhäuser* or the raging sea in *The Flying Dutchman* – it is always the music that sweeps us along by its sheer power and invests the

169 The German actor Ludwig Gabillon as Hagen in Hebbel's (1813–63) drama *Die Nibelungen* (1861). Costume, shield and headdress are very similar to those sketched by Wagner himself for his tetralogy, *The Ring of the Nibelung*.

characters with their fullest meaning. It is by their music that Wagner's music dramas live.

He of course did not see it like this. For him his dramas were *Gesamtkunstwerke* – total fusions of music, poetry, decor, lighting and staging (only in *Tannhäuser* was dance significant). This was before the days of the 'star' producer, and he liked to supervise every detail of the production, either personally or by correspondence. Some of his demands – for the Valkyries on their flying chargers, or the Rhinemaidens guarding their gold – set problems whose visual realization could hardly have been solved before the coming of the cinema. Whatever the inner meaning of his music, the possibility of using stage symbolism seems never to have occurred to him, and he favoured 'realistic' sets, with Tristan navigating a convincing looking ship, Hans Sachs working in an *echt*-medieval Nuremberg, and Klingsor's Magic Garden resplendent with luxuriant botanical specimens.

The reaction against this overdressed stage came after his death. The
*70* most important spokesman was the Swiss Adolphe Appia (1862–1928). Appia revered Wagner's music but was revolted by what he saw at Bayreuth; to him the fussy, cluttered stage was the antithesis of the sublimity of the music. He embodied his ideas in two treatises, *La Mise-en-Scène du drame Wagnérien* (1895) and *Die Musik und die Inszenierung* (1899); the sets which he designed, bald and austere, low in colour value and with emphatic stress on subtlety of lighting, were accepted only slowly, but gradually his ideas spread through Germany and eventually became the basis of Wieland Wagner's post-war Bayreuth productions of his grandfather's works.

Little need be said of Wagner's German contemporaries. Engelbert Humperdinck (1854–1921) performed a seemingly impossible miracle in 1893 with his *Hänsel und Gretel*, a simple nursery story that was subjected to full Wagnerian treatment and survived. Another, earlier adherent of the 'new' music of the 1850s was Peter Cornelius, remembered for his *Der Barbier von Bagdad*. This was the last opera produced by Liszt at Weimar (1858). Flotow's *Martha* (1847) was lighter stuff, as were Hermann Goetz's *The Taming of the Shrew* and Nicolai's *The Merry Wives of Windsor* (1849). The real challenge to Wagner came, not from any of the traditional strongholds, but from a totally unexpected quarter, Russia.

# Opera in England, Spain, Sweden and Eastern Europe, Nationalism

Throughout the nineteenth century Great Britain was an Italian operatic colony. Its chief seat of opera, Covent Garden, was known as *170–171* The Royal Italian Opera House, and here Italian was the reigning language, even for French or German operas. Native composers such as the Irishman Michael Balfe, or naturalized Italians such as Michael Costa, took Italian opera as their model. Even the German-born Julius Benedict, who had spent many years in Naples, came to England with, musically, an Italian accent.

There was no lack of composers (Barnett, Cowen, Goring Thomas, MacCunn, Mackenzie, Stanford, Sullivan, Wallace), and rather more operas were performed than one might think. In London, for example, opera could be heard at Covent Garden, Drury Lane, the Lyceum, the St James's theatre (where there were seasons of French opera in French), the Alhambra and the Grand Theatre, Islington. Provincial towns had to rely on touring companies, of which the Moody-Manners and the Carl Rosa were the best known.

Attempts at establishing English opera on a secure permanent basis were abortive. Balfe tried, and all but succeeded. Opera houses were *172* projected, and some were even built. One of these, the Royal English Opera House, was successfully inaugurated with Sir Arthur Sullivan's only grand opera, *Ivanhoe*, in 1891. The project died, partly because there was no opera ready to follow Sullivan's.

Eric Walter White, in his *The Rise of English Opera*, lists some two hundred first performances of English operas during the nineteenth century. No doubt most of these are deservedly neglected; but how many forgotten Italian or German operas would stand revival? England's case is similar to that of many countries; there was a fair amount of operatic activity, and more native effort than is commonly supposed, but, if we except Sullivan and his comic operas, no talent comparable with *the best* in the international scene.

Spain, for example, has a somewhat similar operatic history. Like England it is separated from the main European centres by a barrier,

but not an impassable one; in one case it is the English Channel, in the other the Pyrenees. Both countries are on a sort of Continental Shelf. Spain, too, had early developed a rich literary and dramatic culture, the work of writers such as Cervantes, Lope de Vega, Calderón de la Barca, Juan del Encina and Tirso de Molina.

Some of these writers participated in the new-fangled entertainments emanating from Italy; for example, a 'pastoral eclogue' was performed at Philip IV's court in 1629. It was by Lope de Vega, and seems to have been sung throughout, though the music is lost; there were 'machines', and an orchestra. Many such entertainments are known. They were performed at the palace known as La Zarzuela, near Madrid – a word perpetuated in the title of Spain's characteristic
*174* type of opera, the *zarzuela*.

170 (*left*) The interior of England's principal opera house, Covent Garden. There has been a theatre on this site since 1732; the present building, replacing one burnt down in 1856, dates from 1858.

171 (*right*) Playbill for Meyerbeer's *Les Huguenots*, the first opera to be presented in the rebuilt Covent Garden opera house.

172 (*below*) A London opera house that might have been: Sir John Soane's impressive and dignified project for an opera house on the north side of Leicester Square. Soane (1753–1837) was an architect and a collector; the house which he designed and built for himself in Lincoln's Inn Fields is now the Sir John Soane Museum, containing much of his work but not this picture, which is in the Museum of London.

# ROYAL ITALIAN OPERA
## COVENT GARDEN.
SEASON, 1858.

MR. GYE HAS THE HONOR TO ANNOUNCE THAT THE

# NEW THEATRE WILL OPEN
# THIS EVENING,
### SATURDAY, MAY 15th, 1858,
ON WHICH OCCASION WILL BE PERFORMED MEYERBEER'S GRAND OPERA, LES

# HUGUENOTS

| | | |
|---|---|---|
| Valentina | - - - | Mad.me GRISI |
| Margarita di Valois | - | Mad.lle MARAI |
| Dama d'onore | - - | Mad.me TAGLIAFICO |
| Urbano - | - - | Mad.lle DIDIEE |
| Marcello | - - | Mons. ZELGER |
| Il Conte di San Bris | - | Sig.r POLONINI |
| Il Conte di Nevers | - | Sig.r TAGLIAFICO |
| Meru | - - - | Sig.r PIERINI |
| Tavannes | - - | Sig.r ROSSI |
| Huguenot Soldier | - | Sig.r SOLDI |
| Raoul di Nangis - | - | Sig.r MARIO |

Conductor - - Mr. COSTA.

AT THE CONCLUSION OF THE OPERA
THE NATIONAL ANTHEM, "GOD SAVE THE QUEEN,"
WILL BE SUNG.
THE INCIDENTAL

# DIVERTISSEMENT
WILL BE SUPPORTED BY
### Mad.lle DELECHAUX,
Mademoiselle ESPER. AND Mons. DESPLACES.

**Doors Open at Half-past SEVEN, the Opera to Commence at EIGHT.**
[R. S. FRANCIS, Printer, Catherine Street, Strand.

A fresh chapter opened in the eighteenth century under Philip V, when an Italian operatic invasion began in earnest. As in England, there was no theatrical personality, musician or playwright, strong enough to withstand it. True, there was no Handel to take command,
59 but in 1737 the *castrato* Farinelli arrived in Madrid, charged with the task of reorganizing the court theatre. This he rebuilt, enlarging the stage 'to take about 150 horses'; he also improved and expanded the orchestra, and during his twenty-two years in Madrid brought the opera to a high pitch of excellence. The repertoire consisted largely of the dramas of his friend Metastasio, set by composers such as Vinci and Jommelli.

After Farinelli left Madrid, the Italian opera flourished intermittently. The fashion for mythological or pastoral subjects, lavishly presented, was followed by a few Spanish composers such as Sebastien Durón, Antonio Literes and Jose de Nebra, but in the second half of the century a more popular type of plot began to appear. The development parallels exactly the similar movements in France,

173 (*left*) The auditorium of the fine Teatro del Liceo, Barcelona.

174 A scene from the *zarzuela La Verbena de la Paloma* ('The Festival of Our Lady of the Dove'), by Tomás Bretón (1850–1923).

Germany and England. Two men may be singled out – the poet Ramon de la Cruz and the composer Rodriguez de Hita. Their pieces, such as *The Reapers of Vallecas* (1768) and *The Working Women of Murcia* (1769), drew on scenes from village life, and the music exploited Spanish songs and dances.

Another development was the rise of the *tonadilla*. Beginning simply as a song, its transformation into a duet or 'dialogue' moved it into the sphere of the dramatic, from whence it evolved into a small operetta lasting ten to twenty minutes, in character not unlike the Neapolitan *intermezzo*. It not only drew on native popular music but used 'types', as in the *commedia dell'arte*, and made lavish use of extempore dialogue and gagging.

This was ephemeral art, written for a day and then forgotten. Some two thousand such works are preserved in Madrid alone. The *tonadilla* did not outlive the eighteenth century, and in fact it was not until well into the 1800s that the Spanish theatre began again to lift up its head.

The centre of the *zarzuela* revival was Madrid, where the Teatro de

Zarzuela was opened in 1856. The moving spirit was Rafael Jose Maria Hernando; other composers associated with him were Emilio Arrieta and Francisco Barbieri. Hernando and Arrieta worked in Italian; Barbieri's works were in Spanish, and more nationalistic in flavour. Spanish folk music is regional – Catalan, Basque, Navarrese, Galician, Andalusian and so on. The music of a true *zarzuela* would be confined to that of the province it was set in, as opposed to, for example, *Carmen*, in which a gipsy from Seville sings a Cuban *habanera* and an Asturian *charrada*.

There are two forms of the *zarzuela* – *zarzuela grande*, an evening's entertainment, in three acts; and *genero chico*, in one act. The latter is usually comic, the former more serious. The composers included Tomás Bretón, some of whose works (for example, *La Verbena de la Paloma*, 1894) travelled as far as Buenos Aires, Joaquín Gaztambide, Ruperto Chapí, Federico Chueca and Geronimo Giminez; they had the co-operation of some of Spain's foremost writers, such as Ventura de la Vega, Carlos Fernandez Shaw, the two Quinteros, Serafin Alvarez and Joaquín Alvarez, and Martinez Sierra.

The *zarzuela* is very little known outside Spain and Latin America but it did have some influence on the work of 'nationalist' composers such as Manuel de Falla, whose *La Vida Breve* (1913) and the charming marionette opera *Master Peter's Puppet Show* (1923) are almost the only Spanish operas to maintain even a precarious foothold internationally.

In Sweden, another 'Continental Shelf' country, the story is similar. There was Italian opera at the Swedish court as early as 1652; then a phase of French influence (Lully, Campra) ensued. A resplendent period began in the 1770s, under Gustav III. An opera house was built in 1782 in which excellent performances of Italian-style operas by Johann Gottlieb Naumann, Gluck and others were given, with first-class decor and costumes by a Frenchman, Louis-Jean
*175* Desprez. This season was cut short by the assassination of the king at a ball given at the opera house – the basis for Auber's *Gustav III* and Verdi's *A Masked Ball*. The opera was resumed under Charles XIII, with a repertory that was largely French (Dalayrac, Boieldieu, Isouard, Méhul; later Spontini, Auber, Meyerbeer) and followed Parisian models in its exotic, monumental settings, inspired by the work of Ciceri, Daguerre and Delacroix. A production of *L'Africaine*, for example, in 1867, with scenery by Ahlgrensson and machinery by

175 A spectacular entertainment at Gripsholm Castle in the time of Gustavus III of Sweden: *La reine Christine*, designed by Louis-Jean Desprez.

Lindström, was regarded as superior to that at the Paris Opéra.

From about 1870 a nationalist movement is recognizable, represented by composers such as Ivar Hallström (*Der Bergtagna*, 1874) and Anders Hallén, whose *Harald the Viking* (Leipzig, 1881) shows German and, more particularly, Wagnerian leanings. But, as in Spain, such operas were mainly of local interest and few have made much headway outside Sweden.

Nationalist stirrings were already apparent in other countries, for instance Hungary, where Ferenc Erkel was working towards a truly national Hungarian opera as early as 1840. His *Bank Ban* (1861) is still performed today. Like Spain, Hungary possessed its own very distinctive style of national music, known as *verbunkos* – dance music, played in a wild, abandoned style, with characteristic rhythms. In Czechoslovakia the comparable figure is Bedřich Smetana, who

176 Act III of *The Bartered Bride*, by Smetana (1824–84), at the Bolshoi theatre, Moscow, 1951, with Chekin as Jeník, Solovyov as Micha, and Maslennikova as Mařenka.

176 composed eight operas; the best is *The Bartered Bride* (1866) – an ingenuous story of village community life decked out with radiant melody, infectious rhythms and sparkling orchestration. The foundations had been laid by František Skroup, who had a true Czech opera performed in 1826. Of Antonín Dvořák's ten operas *Rusalka* (1901) has been on the whole the most successful. Other Czech composers are Zdenek Fibich, Karel Bendl, Josef Bohuslav Foerster, Vitězslav Novák, Otakar Ostrčil and Bohuslav Martinů; but the composer with the most arresting personality is Leoš Janáček. His reputation has grown markedly since his death in 1928. His very personal musical style grows out of and is indissolubly linked to the idiosyncrasies of the Czech language, but this has not hindered the acceptance of his operas abroad: *Jenůfa* (1904), *Katya Kabanová* (1921), *The Cunning Little Vixen* (1924), *The Makropoulos Case* (1926) and *From the House of the Dead* (1930) have all joined the international repertory as undisputed masterpieces of twentieth-century opera.

177 Simple designs, bold features and striking colours continue to be characteristic of Russian theatre design. A set, by Fedor Federowsky, for *Ivan Susanin* (Glinka, 1804–57) at the Kirov theatre, Leningrad, 1940.

Of all the nineteenth-century nationalist groups the most distinctive was the Russian. The early history of opera in Russia is shadowy but becomes clearer in the eighteenth century under the Empress Anna Ivanovna, who in 1735 invited an Italian, Francesco Araja, to her court; but it was the Empress Catherine II (Catherine the Great) who did most to foster the exotic Italian opera. She established a flourishing little Italian colony of singers and players at St Petersburg, and leading composers such as Galuppi, Cimarosa and Paisiello were lured there. She also encouraged native composers to some extent, sending Bortniansky to Italy to study and appointing him Imperial *maestro di cappella* on his return to Russia in 1779.

A further period of artistic subjection, this time to France, followed early in the nineteenth century. Boieldieu, for example, was in Russia from 1803 to 1811 as conductor of the Imperial Opera, and during this time had eight of his works performed there, in French, the official language of the court. The music heard by the young Mikhail Glinka

178 The finale of Glinka's *Ruslan and Ludmilla* at the Bolshoi theatre, Moscow, 1957.

included much of this French repertory – Cherubini's *The Water Carrier*, Méhul's *Joseph*, Boieldieu's *Le Petit Chaperon rouge*.

Glinka's circle included, besides the composer Dargomïzhsky, writers such as Pushkin, Gogol and Zhokovsky. In the early 1830s he went on an extended European tour, returning to Russia in 1833 fired with the desire to write a specifically nationalist opera. Zhokovsky
177 suggested a subject taken from Russian history, and in 1836 Glinka's *Ivan Susanin* ('A Life for the Czar') was presented, with great success.
178 In his second opera, *Ruslan and Ludmilla* (1842), a national style is much more noticeable; while *Ivan Susanin* had been virtually an Italian opera on a Russian theme, with some characteristically Russian features, *Ruslan* has already something of the rough vigour, the broad sweep, the colourful harmony and orchestration that are the distinguishing marks of the later Russian composers, such as Borodin, Mussorgsky and Tchaikovsky.

Glinka's genius was only fitful, nor was he gifted with the force of character to follow up his two successes. The same might be said of Dargomïzhsky, who, in his two operas *Rusalka* (1856) and *The Stone Guest* (produced posthumously in 1872, with orchestration completed by Rimsky-Korsakov), attempted to forge a new musical language based on the inflections of Russian speech, but with not quite the musical genius to carry it through. The vision was realized by Mussorgsky in his magnificent *Boris Godunov* (1874). This, Russian in theme and treatment, owed little to any of the current styles. It rejected the conventional continuously composed acts in favour of a series of self-contained *tableaux* (a practice later followed by Debussy in *Pelléas et Mélisande* and Berg in *Wozzeck*) and was couched in a rough-hewn musical language that scorned the cultivated polish of professionalism. Its 'crudities' of harmony, orchestration and structure were smoothed out by Rimsky-Korsakov, whose version was once preferred in some quarters to Mussorgsky's more rugged and vigorous original. *179, 185, 186*

179 Backcloth by Alexander Golovin (1863–1930) for Diaghilev's 1908 Moscow production of *Boris Godunov*, by Mussorgsky (1839–81).

180 Ivan Bilibin's cover design for the vocal score of Rimsky-Korsakov's *The Golden Cockerel*. This, after difficulties with the censor, was first produced at Zimin's theatre, Moscow, in 1909, after the composer's death.

If Mussorgsky lacked professional competence, Rimsky-Korsakov had an excess of it. Like Mussorgsky, he drew on Russian literature and folklore for his themes, but realism attracted him less than fairy tales and magic. He was especially happy in the treatment of the fantastic, as we can see in *May Night* (1880) or *The Snow Maiden* (1882). His gifts
*180, 181* are seen at their best in his last opera, *The Golden Cockerel* (1909), a scintillating compound of fantasy, colour, comedy and political satire. Tchaikovsky is another composer in whom richness of musical invention and sureness of technique atone for uncertain dramatic instinct. His vein of impassioned lyricism lent itself well to the theme
*188* of *Eugene Onegin* (1879), his masterpiece, but of his ten operas only this work and *The Queen of Spades* (1890) have won general acceptance.

Though the chief operatic centres were the State Theatres in

181 Natalia Goncharova's design for the stage curtain for Rimsky-Korsakov's *The Golden Cockerel*, 1914.

182 The Kirov theatre, Leningrad, which rivals Moscow's Bolshoi theatre in the splendour and richness of its productions. It was built in 1860 as the Maryinsky theatre.

183 The theatre at Tiflis, Georgia, built in 1880.

184 Ossip Petrov (1806–78), one of the greatest Russian basses of the nineteenth century.

185 The superb Feodor Chaliapin (1873–1938) in his most famous role, Boris Godunov, at the Champs-Elysées theatre, Paris, 1913.

Moscow (the Bolshoi, or Grand) and St Petersburg (the Maryinsky, *182*
now renamed the Kirov), much experience of operatic production
was also being gained in other theatres, including some in the *183*
provinces. There were private theatres, as, for instance, that of Prince Yussupov, where the performers were often drawn from the serfs on the big estates. There were other private (that is, commercial) theatres in the cities, as, for example, that built by the rich Moscow manufacturer, Mamentov, where works such as *Faust* and *Aida* were performed.

Mamentov is important for his patronage of native talent; it was he
who gave the famous bass Chaliapin his first opportunity to sing *185*
Russian operas in Russian. He also encouraged scenic designers; two of
his protégés, Golovin and Korovin, were snapped up by Volkonsky, *179, 188*
the Director of the Imperial Theatres. Their designs for *Swan Lake*,

186 Set by Léon Bakst (1886–1925) for Diaghilev's 1913 Paris production of Mussorgsky's *Boris Godunov*.

*Eugene Onegin*, *Carmen*, *Boris Godunov* and other works showed that vigorous use of massed primary colours revealed by the more familiar
*186* Ballets Russes designers, Léon Bakst and Alexander Benois. Another important private theatre was that owned by Simin, who also set out
*177, 187* deliberately to encourage young Russian designers such as
*180, 189, 190* Federowsky, Bilibin, Polenov, Yegerov, Roerich and Sudeikin.

During the years leading up to the First World War and the 1917 Revolution the Russian theatre was in a healthy state of ferment, producing ideas and experiments that have not lost their validity today. In about 1912, for instance, Mardshanov, a wealthy amateur, created what he called 'synthetic theatre': he demanded that the player should be universal – dancer, singer, actor, acrobat. This idea was developed further by Alexander Tairov, who in the autumn of 1914

187 Costume designs (1913) by Federowsky for Mussorgsky's *Khovanchina*, an opera left unfinished at the composer's death. It was completed by Rimsky-Korsakov, and first performed in 1886.

188, 189, 190 *Above:* Curtain design by Alexander Golovin for a production of Tchaikovsky's *Eugene Onegin* at the Kirov theatre, Leningrad, 1926. *Opposite:* Sets by Nicolas Roerich for the 1909 Bolshoi theatre production of *Prince Igor*, by Borodin (1833–87).

opened the Moscow Kamerny, or Chamber, Theatre. There the theatrical technique was to be neither naturalistic nor stylistic; Tairov maintained that the literary play was the enemy of histrionic art, that the true road to salvation lay through the old *commedia dell'arte* and improvisation. Many of these ideas strikingly anticipate some present-day thoughts in connection with 'total theatre' (see page 239), but the opera of the time proved less amenable to these unconventional ideas than the sister art of ballet, which was on the eve of regeneration under the inspiring lead of Diaghilev.

With the Revolution came a new philosophy; opera had to work for its living. Hitched to a propaganda wagon, it gave rise to some strange distortions, as for instance Puccini's *Tosca*, rewritten as *The Fight for the Commune* and with the scene laid in the Paris of 1871, or *The Huguenots*, reworked as *The Decembrists* and set in St Petersburg in 1825 (not to be confused with Shaporin's *The Decembrists*, 1953).

191 Costume design by Isaac Rabinovich for Prokofiev's *Love for Three Oranges*, Moscow, 1927.

## Opera in the New World

Since the period of rising prosperity in the developing countries of the New World was the time of the height of the European craze for Italian opera, and since the great colonizing nations, England, Spain and Portugal, all lacked strong native operatic traditions, so it came about that Latin America, colonized by Spain and Portugal, favoured Italian opera from the start, while North America, overcoming with some reluctance its puritanical suspicion of the theatre, found itself in the nineteenth century veering towards the German camp by reason of an influx of German immigrants. In both North and South America serious composers seem to have been drawn to instrumental and symphonic composition rather than to opera. Carlos Chavez, for example, Mexico's most distinguished composer, wrote no operas: Brazil's Villa-Lobos wrote five, but only *Yerma* (1955) has been performed.

There were opera houses in Brazil in the eighteenth century, but an extra stimulus was given when the Portuguese court was exiled to Rio de Janeiro in 1808. Here John VI set up a musical establishment on the European model, with mainly Italian singers and players. A national opera was instituted in 1857, with a repertory that included Spanish *zarzuelas* and a few operas by Brazilian composers who drew on Europe, again largely Italy, for their inspiration rather than on their own rich heritage of folk song and dance. Carlos Gomez (1836–96), for example, wrote an opera, *Il Guarany*, to a story by the Brazilian writer José Alencar; but the libretto was in Italian, and it was first produced in 1870 in Milan. The Italian language was the rule; the first Brazilian opera in Portuguese was not produced until 1901; this was *A Noite de São João* ('St John's Eve'), by Elias Alvares Lobo (1834–1901).

A prolific composer whose one opera, *Malzarte* (1941), though written to an Italian libretto, gets nearer to the heart of Brazil, is Oscar Lorenzo Fernandez. This unites something like the Wagnerian *Leitmotiv* principle with Brazilian folk song and dance. Francisco Mignone is another composer whose large output includes operas that

192 The interior of South America's most important opera house, the Teatro Colón, Buenos Aires

manage to combine Italian libretti with Brazilian music, as for example *The Diamond Merchant* (1922) and *L'Innocente* (1928).

In Argentina a regular opera company was established in about 1823; the first complete opera to be given there was Rossini's *The*
192 *Barber of Seville*, in 1825. The present Teatro Colón (Buenos Aires), one of the world's leading opera houses and the successor to two previous theatres, was opened in 1908 with *Aida*. It has always maintained a close rapport with Milan's La Scala; the native-born Ettore Panizza (1875–1967) was trained there and his own operas (*The Bride of the Sea*, 1897; *Arora*, 1908) upheld the Italian tradition. Other Argentinian composers include Constantino Gaito, Juan Bautista Massa and Alfredo Schiuma. Arturo Berutti, who studied in Germany and Italy, wrote some operas which dealt with events in his own country (for example, *Los Heroes*, 1919); his pupil Felipe Boero's *Tucuman*, produced at the Teatro Colón in 1918, broke new ground

193 The Spanish soprano Isabel Perragos as Julia Farnese (Bomarzo's wife) in the first performance, in the Lisner Auditorium, Washington, D.C., of Ginastera's *Bomarzo*.

by having a Spanish libretto, and the same composer's most popular and widely played work, *El Matrero* (1929), employed Argentinian folk material. Very little of this operatic music has been exported, though some has been played in Italy.

An Argentinian composer whose music was less derivative in style is Alberto Ginastera (1916–83). Like most of his compatriots, he seemed happier in any medium other than opera, but his *Bomarzo* remains the most distinctive Argentinian opera to date. It was commissioned by the Opera Society of Washington, D.C., performed there for the first time on 19 May 1967, and subsequently mounted by the New York City Opera and the New Opera Company in London, with a certain success. Its first performance in Argentina was scheduled for August 1967, but the censorship raised objections and it was banned 'to protect public morality'.

In 1827 Mexico enjoyed a visit by an opera company under Manuel

Garcia, the founder of a dynasty of singers and the father of two of the
132 nineteenth century's most brilliant stars, Maria Malibran and Pauline
Viardot-Garcia. (Two years earlier the same troupe had been to New York.) A little later the Spanish composer Gaztambide took light opera (Offenbach) and *zarzuelas* to Mexico and thus started a fashion for the lighter forms which were cultivated by the Mexican composers Ernest Elordny, José Austin and Luis Arcarez. Other nineteenth-century Mexican composers were Melesio Morales, who used Romani's libretto for a *Romeo y Julieta* (1863), and Aniceto Ortega, whose *Guatimotzin* (1871) was the first Mexican opera to be based on Mexican history. Twentieth-century Mexican composers have shown on the whole little inclination towards the form.

Opera in the United States also began by relying heavily on Europe, all composers, conductors, singers and impresarios being imported. The trade balance on the performing side has altered considerably during the present century, with American artists firmly established in the international ranks; but an opera by an American composer is still a rarity in the European opera house (discounting, for the moment, the 'musical').

For most opera lovers the first name in American opera is
194 'Metropolitan'; but this famous house, opened in 1883 and now
195 demolished (though the name has been given to a new building), had a
number of distinguished precursors, the grandest and most sumptuous being the Academy of Music, opened in 1854. A rival to the
196 Metropolitan was the Manhattan Opera House, which mounted some
very impressive opera seasons under Oscar Hammerstein I (grandfather of the writer of lyrics and musical 'books') from 1907 onwards, until it was bought off by the 'Met'.

Among other American cities, Boston has enjoyed opera seasons, in various languages, since the mid-nineteenth century, though it did not acquire a custom-built opera house (now destroyed) until the twentieth century. Chicago was early in the American field, with an opera house built in 1865; but the transplant flowered only sporadically (there was a brilliant period early this century under the
223 inspiration of Mary Garden) and now exists as a carefully tended
hothouse plant in the 'international' season. New Orleans, naturally, encouraged a French repertory, while in the Far West there are long international seasons at San Francisco, in the War Memorial Opera House, opened in 1932. Regular international seasons also take place at

194, 195 The crowded auditorium at the opening night (the opera performed was Gounod's *Faust*) of the last season of the old New York Metropolitan, before the move in 1966 to new premises in the Lincoln Center (*below*).

Houston, Philadelphia, Los Angeles, Dallas, Cincinnati and Seattle. There are now many summer festivals ranging from the international at Santa Fé to more domestic undertakings, such as the seasons by The Opera Theatre of St. Louis, where performances of quality are given by a young, tight-knit ensemble.

Operas by American composers were few before the present century. There was a curious anticipation of *William Tell*, *The Archers, or Mountaineers of Switzerland*, in 1796, and an attempt at 'grand opera', *Leonora*, in 1845. The Metropolitan stronghold was first breached by an American composer with Frederick Shepherd Converse's *Pipe of Desire* in 1910, and the following decades saw the appearance of quite a school of composers – Charles Wakefield Cadman (*Shanewis*, on a Red Indian theme, 1918), Henry Hadley (*Azora, Daughter of Montezuma*, 1917), Deems Taylor (*Peter Ibbetson*, 1931) and Howard Hanson (*Merry Mount*, 1934). None of these works did much more than echo the contemporary European conventions.

196 (*left*) The Manhattan Opera House on West 34th Street, New York. It was built by Oscar Hammerstein I (1846–1919), and it opened in 1906 with Bellini's *I Puritani*.

197 The American baritone Lawrence Tibbett (1896–1960) as Emperor Jones in the opera of that name by Louis Gruenberg (1884–1964), at the Metropolitan, New York, 1933.

Nevertheless, winds of change were beginning to blow through the operatic corridors. The barriers between serious and light music were beginning to crumble; jazz and black American music increasingly invaded musical life; there was the impact of the 'talkies', which at once became 'singies'; and, finally, the excellence of teaching centres such as the New York Juilliard School of Music was encouraging a new generation of composers who never went abroad to study. Among these were George Antheil (*Transatlantic*, 1930) and Louis Gruenberg, whose *Emperor Jones*, based on Eugene O'Neill's play, was *197* produced at the Metropolitan in 1933 and had several European performances. These works, with Marc Blitzstein's *The Cradle Will Rock* (1937), belonged to the 'experimental' theatre of the 1930s; they represented reaction against 'grand' opera, and were influenced by comparable experiments in Germany, notably the Brecht/Weill *Die Dreigroschenoper* ('The Threepenny Opera', 1928) and Ernst Krenek's *Jonny spielt auf* ('Johnny strikes up', 1927).

198 A scene from Virgil Thomson's *Four Saints in Three Acts*, from the first staging in the Avery Memorial theatre, Hartford, Connecticut, 1934.

199 (*below*) A scene from Gershwin's opera, *Porgy and Bess*, first produced in Boston, Massachusetts, in 1935.

200 Design by Franco Zeffirelli for *Antony and Cleopatra*, by Samuel Barber (b. 1910). This was the first opera produced at the new Metropolitan Opera House, New York, 1966.

Other composers such as Aaron Copland and Virgil Thomson continued the pilgrimage to Europe but took the then fashionable route to Paris, to study with the great teacher Nadia Boulanger. In Paris Thomson met the writer Gertrude Stein, whose style was at that time considered very advanced and eccentric. His collaboration with her yielded the unusual and strangely beautiful *Four Saints in Three* 198
*Acts* (1934), one of the most individual scores written by an American up to that time.

In the following year George Gershwin (1898–1937), in *Porgy and* 199
*Bess*, achieved the most convincing amalgam to date of the various elements of the emerging indigenous American theatre. The work also focused attention sharply on the American black; it demands our sympathy for the crippled Porgy and his sweetheart Bess, caught in the twin toils of society's callousness and their own frailty. The first of the Italian-born Gian Carlo Menotti's series of operas, *Amelia Goes to*

*the Ball*, was produced at about this time (1937). Menotti, who both produces and writes libretti for other composers as well as himself, is one of the most vital theatre men of our time. His view is the Italian one, that the theatre should entertain, which he does with Grand Guignol (*The Medium*), comedy (*The Telephone*), sentiment (the television opera *Amahl and the Night Visitors*) and passionate drama
201 (*The Consul*). Critics are often censorious, finding a dross of cheap sensationalism in his music.

Since the 1930s, and more particularly since the Second World War, activity has intensified, on a scale and with a variety that will astonish anyone who regards the United States as simply a distant outpost of the European operatic empire. The Metropolitan is, of course, a great opera house, with the standards expected of the dozen or so great houses of the world. But, for every first performance of an American opera at the Metropolitan (for example, Samuel Barber's *Vanessa*, 1958), scores of others are given throughout this great country. Interestingly enough, they are subsidized – but the subsidy is hidden. The twentieth-century equivalent of the town theatres of Germany or Italy is the drama department of the American college or university. In 1955, according to the music critic Olin Downes (in *Opera Annual*, 1955–56), there were more than seven hundred separate operatic enterprises in existence in the United States; and between 1930 and 1967 more than a thousand American operas were written. A brief survey of opera can do no more than note this fact, except to observe that, if sheer numbers mean anything, opera in the New World is no more in its death throes than it is in Europe.

201 Patricia Neway as Magda in the first performance of Menotti's *The Consul*, Philadelphia, 1950.

# Operetta, Musical Comedy and the Musical

Nineteenth-century operetta was a combination of a sentimental or romantic story told in spoken dialogue, music and dancing, which aimed to divert rather than to edify. It was a French growth, its roots going back to the early days of *opéra-comique*. The tradition of light musical entertainment then established continued in the works of eighteenth-century composers such as Grétry, Monsigny and Philidor. Their music was akin to that of musical comedy in pace and delicacy of texture; Offenbach himself acknowledged that they possessed these qualities, and regarded himself as belonging to the same tradition. But in the nineteenth century the distinction between 'opera' and the lighter 'operetta' became sharper. 'Opera', the more serious art form, was now universally sung throughout, and it was this attitude that led to *Carmen*, technically an *opéra-comique* in that it originally had spoken dialogue, being officially elevated to the rank of 'opera' by having this spoken dialogue converted into recitatives (which were supplied by the French composer Ernest Guiraud).

The distinction did not, however, become clear-cut until Offenbach's time. An Italian influence has already been noted in the music of such composers as Boieldieu and Auber, which extends also to their lighter works. Boieldieu's *Le Calife de Bagdad* (1800) and Auber's *Fra Diavolo* (1830), though they are the spiritual heirs of the French eighteenth-century *opéra-comique* tradition, lean towards 'opera' by virtue of their rather more elaborate musical organization. Other French composers during the first half of the nineteenth century whose works hovered on the borders between opera and operetta were Adolphe Adam, whose *Le Postillon de Longjumeau* (1836) is a delightful example of French light opera of this period, Albert Grisar (*Pantalon*, 1851), Antoine Louis Clapisson (*La Franchonnette*, 1856), Louis Aimé Maillart (*Les Dragons de Villars*, 1856) and Victor Massé (*Galateé*, 1852; *Les Noces de Jeanette*, 1853). Their works, unpretentious and rather frivolous, prepared the way for the full flowering of the operetta in the more favourable atmosphere of the Second Empire (1852–70).

202 Set by Yves-Bonnat for the 1955 Paris production of Messager's *Monsieur Beaucaire*.

203, 204 Costume designs, by G. Jacouloff, for Alexander Tairov's production of Lecocq's *Giroflé-Girofla* at the Moscow Kamerny theatre, 1922.

205, 206, 207 Costume designs by Ernst Stern for a production of *The Merry Widow*, Berlin, 1927.

This was dominated by Jacques Offenbach (1819–80). Born in Cologne, the son of a Jewish cantor (his real name was Jakob Eberst), he was early taken by his father to Paris, where we find him at the age of fourteen at the Conservatoire, studying the cello. His true bent, however, was for composition, his ambition, opera; but entry into the circle of Parisian theatre life proved far from easy. The theatres were still tightly organized, to a scheme laid down by Napoleon Bonaparte, which stipulated the type of 'spectacle' each theatre might present and which limited the smaller theatres to no more than four players. Some of the expedients used by Offenbach to outwit officialdom were as resourceful and amusing as the antics of the earlier Fair players recounted in Chapter Three. He battled against the establishment, and his first successes were in what might be called 'off Broadway' theatres – if indeed they deserved the name of theatre at all, so small were they. His energy was inexhaustible. He was not only composer and conductor, but copyist, stage manager and impresario all at once. He had a flair for talent-spotting. One of his protégées was the actress
*209* Hortense Schneider; he early recognized the literary gifts of Ludovic Halévy, and a composition competition which he organized brought to light two young men who later made their mark in the French
*202–4* theatre. They were Charles Lecocq, who with André Messager and others continued the French operetta tradition, and Georges Bizet.

Offenbach's first theatre was a tiny wooden structure on the

208 (*left*) Valerie Masterson as Eurydice in Offenbach's *Orpheus in the Underworld*; a production by Sadler's Wells Opera at the London Coliseum, 1968.

209 (*right*) Hortense Schneider (1833–1920) as the Duchess in Offenbach's *La Grande Duchesse de Gérolstein* (1867).

210 (*below*) The can-can from Offenbach's *La vie parisienne*, in Jean-Louis Barrault's production at the Odéon, Paris, 1959–60.

Champs-Elysées, near the 1855 World Exhibition, opened that year under the name Bouffes-Parisiens; it was exchanged later in the year for another, almost as small, on the Boulevard des Italiens. Here in 1857 he had his first resounding success, *Orphée aux Enfers*, an *208* extraordinarily clever skit on Gluck's *Orphée*. An astonishing series of works followed, in all nearly a hundred: witty, satirical, up to date, parodying more serious music and musicians, pricking the bubble of pomposity. Among the better known are *La Belle Hélène* (1864), *La Vie parisienne* (1866) and *La Grande Duchesse de Gérolstein* (1867). His *209, 210* last and most ambitious work, *Les Contes d'Hoffman* (1881), is a romantic opera and in quite a different category.

211 Karl Adolf Friese as the Prison Governor, and Alfred Schreiber as Frosch, in the original production of *Die Fledermaus*, by Johann Strauss, Vienna, 1874.

Offenbach's fame, and his music, soon spread beyond Paris, to London and to Vienna, the city that was to become the home of operetta *par excellence*. Vienna had had its own tradition of light opera or *Singspiel*, cultivated by such composers as Conradin Kreutzer and the prolific Wenzel Müller. But by 1861, when Offenbach went there, they were both dead, and only Suppé in the next generation seemed to have either the enthusiasm or the flair for this lighter genre.

The challenge of Offenbach's Parisian successes was taken up by Johann Strauss the younger (1825–99), already a composer of repute when he made his first tentative moves towards the opera house. Two operettas, *Indigo* and *Karnaval in Rom*, Both mounted by Maximilian Steiner at the famous Theater an der Wien, went off at half cock. Then, in 1874, appeared the work that is still as alive today as at its first
211 performance – *Die Fledermaus*, based like so many others on a Parisian success, *Reveillon*, by Offenbach's collaborators Meilhac and Halévy.

The dozen or so operettas that followed never quite matched this

212 Mizzi Günther and Louis Treumann in the first performance of Lehar's *The Merry Widow*, Vienna, 1905. This operetta, like *Die Fledermaus*, was based on a French comedy by Meilhac.

first success, though *The Gipsy Baron* (1885) ran it a close second. Through them all the Viennese waltz runs like a motto; the roots of Viennese operetta took their nourishment from the dancing Congress of 1815 and the waltzes of Lanner and Strauss *père*. And while Offenbach, a little like Rossini, entertains us by his exuberance, his wit, his irreverence, the Viennese breathe a softer air; the appeal of Strauss and his followers is unashamedly to the heart, the laughter is more affectionate, the humour less astringent.

Strauss's successor kept Vienna supplied with a stream of nostalgic confections right up to the outbreak of the First World War. Franz Lehár (1870–1948) was from Hungary, and added a fresh touch to the Viennese colouring; his *The Merry Widow* (1905) has been accorded full classical status, and granted the accolade of sumptuous and distinguished productions in some of the world's leading houses. In Leo Fall's *The Dollar Princess* (1907) and Oscar Straus's *The Chocolate Soldier* (1908), based on G.B. Shaw's *Arms and the Man*, the illusion of

*205–7, 212*

the carefree, dancing Austria continued to be fostered, and indeed a world that trembled on the brink of disaster, and was finally plunged headlong into it, utterly refused to renounce its daydreams in the theatre. While Paris remained incorrigibly 'naughty', Vienna obstinately refused to stop waltzing.

The Viennese recipe proved particularly enticing in London, which took *The Merry Widow*, *The Dollar Princess*, *Gipsy Love* (Lehár) and *The Chocolate Soldier* rapturously to its bosom. After the First World War the liaison, with Berlin as well as Vienna, was resumed with *Lilac Time*, *The Last Waltz* (Berlin, 1920) and other operettas, competing in splendour of production with the Cochran revues. The culminating
213 extravaganza was *The White Horse Inn* (first produced in Berlin, 1930), before the combination of the Depression and the sound-film pronounced the death sentence on the 'colossal' show.

Victorian England seems on the whole to have preferred Parisian spice to Viennese cake. French operetta could be heard at several theatres, notably the St James's (Offenbach brought his troupe there in 1857); the Gaiety, famed for its musical comedies under the management of George Edwardes; the Lyceum, where some of
214 Hervé's pieces, such as *Chilpéric* and *Le petit Faust*, were given; and the

213 (*left*) A production of *The White Horse Inn* at the London Coliseum, 1931. The scenery and costumes were designed by Ernst Stern. The scenery overflowed from the stage into the boxes – an attempt at involving the audience that seems to have anticipated later developments such as Cinerama.

214 Emily Soldene, a much-loved Victorian stage personality. She sang in both opera and musical comedy. She is seen here as Chilpéric in Hervé's comic opera of that name (Lyceum, London, 1870).

Alhambra, which for several years from about 1871 staged *opéra bouffe* in a very competent manner.

This is the context in which we must see the Savoy operas. Gilbert's particular brand of topsy-turvy libretto, founded on the English burlesque tradition exploited by J.R. Planché and F.C. Burnand, is nearer in spirit to Paris than Vienna. His comedy was verbal; the absurd situations in which his characters found themselves would be underlined by the apt work or the pointed phrase. His handling of the outrageous pun or the far-fetched rhyme links him with other verbal humorists of the time, such as Lewis Carroll or Edward Lear. Sullivan, for all his worship at the shrines of Schumann and Wagner while he was a student at Leipzig, brought a lightness of touch and a transparency of texture that are closer to Rossini and Offenbach, and intentionally so; for the operettas which he wrote in conjunction with Gilbert were frankly in competition with the Parisian successes of the day, such as *The Grand Duchess of Gerolstein*, or Lecocq's *La Fille de Madame Angot*, which caused just as much of a sensation in London as they had caused in Paris. He improved on his models, and the succession of Savoy operettas that began with *The Sorcerer* in 1877 – *H.M.S. Pinafore*, *The Pirates of Penzance*, *Patience*, *Iolanthe*, *The*

215 Marie Tempest (1864–1942), who was well established as a singer before she embarked on her career as a comedy actress, in *The Geisha*, by Sidney Jones. *The Geisha*, first produced in 1896, had a run of over two years, and was for generations the standby of amateur operatic societies.

216 *Mikado*, *The Yeomen of the Guard* and *The Gondoliers* – were fashioned of an enduring substance which has so far resisted decay.

After the Second World War the Viennese operetta experienced a transatlantic metamorphosis. A new self-confidence and a more virile optimism replaced the febrile gaiety and the nostalgic harping on an imaginary past Golden Age; the American musical was born.

Song-and-dance shows, in which a bevy of chorus girls was the main attraction, were already well established in nineteenth-century America, and the links between these and the Viennese operetta which had been forged by the number of Teutonic immigrants who had settled in New York and Chicago were further strengthened when three European composers made their homes in the New World. They were the Irishman Victor Herbert, the Czech Rudolf Friml and the Hungarian Sigmund Romberg. Their fairy-tale romances fitted Dr Johnson's famous definition of opera as an 'exotic and irrational entertainment' quite well: Friml's *The Vagabond King* was set in fifteenth-century France, Romberg's *The Student Prince* in some mythical Ruritania, his *Desert Song* in North Africa – all far removed from twentieth-century America.

But already there was a move towards home ground and a less escapist type of story. America had its own romance, its own brand of nostalgia. It also had its own problems – the poor, and particularly the Negro poor. These ideas found expression in the first great American musical, *Show Boat* (1927). The book and lyrics, based on the novel by Edna Ferber, were by Oscar Hammerstein II, and the music was by the American-born Jerome Kern. *Show Boat* was staged by Florenz Ziegfeld, the impresario of the noted 'Ziegfeld Follies' which enlivened New York theatre life for over twenty years.

Kern was one of a group of composers – Irving Berlin, Cole Porter, George Gershwin, Richard Rodgers and others – who between them established the American musical as a typically transatlantic theatre form which, at its best, is a combination of music, song, decor and

216 The first-act finale of Gilbert and Sullivan's *The Mikado*; a production by the D'Oyly Carte company in Birmingham, 1966.

217 *Oklahoma!*, by Richard Rodgers and Oscar Hammerstein. A scene from the original 1943 Broadway production.

dance not unlike opera as originally conceived in seventeenth-century
217 Italy. The success of such works as *Pal Joey*, *Oklahoma!*, *The King and I*, *Kiss Me, Kate*, *Guys and Dolls*, *Annie Get Your Gun*, *My Fair Lady* and a host of others depended on team work between composer, authors such as Oscar Hammerstein, Lorenz Hart and Guy Bolton, and choreographers like George Balanchine, Agnes de Mille and Jerome Robbins, coupled with first-class costuming and staging.

The 'musical' has been hailed in some quarters as America's contribution to opera. Not everyone would concede this, but in the best examples – by composers such as Kurt Weill (*Lady in the Dark*, *Street Scene*), Leonard Bernstein (*On the Town*, *West Side Story*) and Stephen Sondheim (*Company*, *A Little Night Music*, *Sweeney Todd*) – there is a vitality and copiousness of invention that make up an art form superior to much that has passed for opera on the stages of the Old World in times both past and present.

CHAPTER FOURTEEN

# Opera in the Twentieth Century

Wagner, said Debussy, was a beautiful sunset that was mistaken for a dawn. But composers in general were slow to shake themselves free from Wagner's influence. The symphonic commentary synthesized by means of a tissue of leading motifs seemed to offer a sure formula for success, which all too often proved illusory. As with the fragments of Siegfried's sword, a master craftsman was needed to forge them into a unity.

The only composer to work on Wagner's heroic scale and to accept the Wagnerian premises without being submerged by them was
Richard Strauss (1864–1949), whose fifteen operas offer a compen- 222
dium of the moods and intentions of twentieth-century music theatre. The first, *Guntram* (1894), is the only one with a theme that might be called Wagnerian; it is set in thirteenth-century Germany, with a strong 'redemption through love' motive running through it.

218 One of Salvador Dali's designs for Peter Brook's controversial production of Richard Strauss's *Salome* at Covent Garden, 1947.

219 Sena Jurinac as Oktavian in Richard Strauss's *Der Rosenkavalier*.

220 (*below*) Murray Dickie as the Dancing Master, Mattiwilda Dobbs as Zerbinetta, Sesto Bruscantini as the Music Master and Sena Jurinac as the Composer in Richard Strauss's *Ariadne auf Naxos*, Glyndebourne, 1953.

221 Maria Jeritza, Strauss's choice for the title role in the first performance of *Ariadne auf Naxos* at Stuttgart, 1912.

222 Richard Strauss, aged thirty.

*Feuersnot* (1901) is a comedy, admixed with allegory and didacticism. The 1905 study in morbidity, *Salome*, kept very close to Oscar Wilde's 218
successful play, first performed in Paris in 1894 and subsequently repeated in many Continental countries, though it was still banned in London. In 1909 came the first of the collaborations with Hugo von Hofmannsthal, *Elektra*, like so many modern operas inspired by the ever-fertile region of Greek mythology. For many the next opera, *Der Rosenkavalier* (1911), ranks as Strauss's masterpiece. Both Strauss and 219
Hofmannsthal intended this to be Mozartian, and indeed the main characters can trace their lineage back to the stock figures of eighteenth-century comedy, but the score is rich and opulent in the typical Strauss manner, with abundant references to the luscious Viennese waltzes of Johann Strauss's time.

For *Ariadne auf Naxos* Hofmannsthal went to Molière's *Le Bourgeois* 220, 221
*Gentilhomme*. This mixed genre, play and opera, left the first audiences nonplussed, but it has found imitators in some of the experimental theatre of the 1960s. The elaborate allegory of *Die Frau ohne Schatten* (1919) was also something that later composers, such as Michael Tippett in *The Midsummer Marriage* (1955), were to explore 247

further. *Intermezzo* (1924) is a curious fragment of autobiographical reportage before television had made such pranks fashionable. The return to Greek myth in *Die Ägyptische Helena* (1928), portentous with meaning, was followed by *Arabella* (1933), a sort of Viennese salon-comedy. *Die schweigsame Frau* (1935) takes Ben Jonson's *Epicoene* as its starting point. Hofmannsthal had died in 1929, and the libretto for this was by Stefan Zweig. But by now the Nazis were in power, and Zweig *persona non grata*, and the next three libretti were by Josef Gregor. *Friedenstag* (1938) is a politico-military opera, an indictment of the military mind, while in *Daphne* (1938) Gregor intended to present 'a tale of man's reconciliation with nature, a mythological equivalent of man's reconciliation with man in *Friedenstag*' (William Mann). *Die Liebe der Danae* (1952, but written much earlier) preaches the emptiness of modern materialism, while in his last opera, *Capriccio* (1942), Strauss and his librettist, the conductor Clemens Krauss, embarked on philosophical discussions over the relation between words and music in opera.

This variety of tragedy, comedy, symbolism, morality, satire and philosophy was no doubt more than one man could comfortably handle, and it is a sign of vitality in twentieth-century opera that such themes, and others, could be acceptable in the opera house. It is interesting to note that appreciation of Strauss's post-*Rosenkavalier* operas, many of which were misunderstood when they first appeared, has steadily advanced since his death.

In any event it was impossible for the lyric theatre to remain indifferent to the 'new' theatre of Ibsen, Shaw, Chekhov, d'Annunzio, Yeats, Hofmannsthal, Maeterlinck and others. In their varied ways they reacted against the conventional naturalism, the externalization, of the nineteenth-century theatre. Instead they searched for inner motives, for truths behind the façade; many of them revived the poetic drama, and sought an enriched experience by the aid of symbolism and an allusive suggestiveness of language.

These are dramatic and poetic areas where music has much of significance to offer, and this was demonstrated to perfection in
*223, 224* Debussy's *Pelléas et Mélisande* (1902). It is a setting, almost intact, of a play by Maurice Maeterlinck, whose works have furnished material for more than a dozen operas. Debussy kept the play's structure of separate and distinct scenes, but 'through-composed' the music. His score is a unique distillation of the essence of Wagner, yielding a new

223, 224 Mary Garden as Mélisande and Jean Alexis Périer as Pelléas in Debussy's *Pelléas et Mélisande* (Paris, Opéra-Comique, 1902). The choice of the Scottish Mary Garden as Mélisande was the cause of a rift between the composer and Maeterlinck, who had believed that his wife was to sing the part.

and purer product, purged of coarseness and over-emphasis, and for many it is the embodiment of that 'drama through music' dreamed of by the Florentine Camerata.

Nor could the arts ignore the new, fashionable interest in psychology. Freud's *The Interpretation of Dreams* was published in 1895, but it only made explicit what the creative artist had always been instinctively aware of, namely, the dominance of the subconscious over the conscious. Music's relevance to abnormal psychological states has been recognized at least since David played to Saul, but music had now to hand a tool of vastly increased potentiality for the illumination of such states, which psychology was suggesting were less abnormal than had been supposed. The lurid quality of Wilde's *Salome* is intensified almost to the point of revulsion by Strauss's treatment; and everywhere as the new century advanced, from Bartók's *Bluebeard's Castle* (completed in 1911, but not produced until 1918) to Janáček's *The House of the Dead* (1930) and Britten's *The Turn of the Screw* (Venice, 1954), we find music, using new and sometimes previously untried techniques, seeking to probe the hidden recesses of the mind.

In at least one instance, Alban Berg's *Wozzeck* (Berlin, 1925), the result is an undisputed masterpiece. The opera is based on an extraordinary play by the nineteenth-century Georg Büchner, whose death in 1837 at the age of twenty-four robbed Germany of one of its most gifted playwrights. The story could not be more anti-heroic: the dull soldier Wozzeck, the butt of his superior officer's sadistic humour, subjected to indignities by the half-crazy medical officer and goaded by the wide-boy sergeant-major, is finally driven by jealousy to the murder of his sluttish woman, Marie; his own end is an ignominious one, by drowning. Berg's music, a compound of atonal and traditional techniques, enfolds this pathetic slice of life with transcendental compassion. His second opera, *Lulu*, was left incomplete at his death in 1935; his widow forbade the realization of the
225 short score of Act III, but following her death Friedrich Cerha's

225 Countess Geschwitz (Brigitte Fassbaender) flirts with Lulu (Catherine Malfitano) in Jean-Pierre Ponnelle's 1985 Munich Opera production of the three-act version of Berg's opera. The conductor, Friedrich Cerha, was also responsible for the completion.

226 The people worshipping the Golden Calf; a scene from the first production of Schoenberg's *Moses and Aaron*, Zurich, 1957.

completion of this expressionist masterpiece was successfully premiered in 1979.

Berg was both pupil and friend of Arnold Schoenberg (1874–1951), who, as might be expected, given his temperament and his background in the Vienna of Freud, Kandinsky, Kafka and Kokoschka, was anything but conformist, and his first two operas were unconventional in form, style and material. Each is less than half an hour long. *Erwartung* ('Expectation'), written in 1909 but not performed until 1924, has one character only, a woman; *Die glückliche Hand* ('The Lucky Hand'), dating from the same time but also not performed until 1924, has one singing part (male), two mimed parts and a chorus. Both works explore states of mind, much as did Bartók's contemporary *Bluebeard's Castle*.

Soon after this Schoenberg, whose music had already lost touch with even the free tonality of *Tristan* and his own tone-poem *Verklärte Nacht* ('Transfigured Night'), evolved the system of composing with twelve notes with which his name is associated. This, referred to variously as 'dodecaphonic music' or 'serialism', was at first confined

to, or at least centred on, the group of composers gathered round him in Vienna – Berg, Krenek, Webern and Wellesz; after the Second World War the technique was widely used, though its influence had begun to wane by the late 1960s. In 1930 Schoenberg experimented with it in a comic opera, *Von Heute auf Morgen* ('From Day to Day'), a domestic *fracas* between husband and wife, with a happy ending
226 While at work on this he had already begun his great *Moses und Aron*, which remained incomplete at his death and was not staged until 1957. The essential theme of the libretto, by the composer himself, is again a philosophical one – the great gulf fixed between the uncompromising ideals of the prophet and visionary (Moses) and the inevitable distortions arising from the attempts by the popularizing spokesman (Aaron) to transmit this message to the people in general.

While Strauss, Berg and Schoenberg worked in an extension of the nineteenth-century German, largely Wagnerian, tradition, other composers were reacting against this orchestra-dominated, through-composed type of music. The leader was the independent-minded Igor Stravinsky (1882–1971), who, after the easily classifiable ballets *Firebird*, *Petrushka* and *The Rite of Spring*, produced some stage works that could not be so readily pigeon-holed, such as *Renard*, written in 1916–17, 'a burlesque tale, to be sung and played', and *The Soldier's Tale* (1918), 'to be read, played and danced'. In the latter, portions of the text were declaimed rhythmically, over the orchestra, in a manner reminiscent of eighteenth-century 'melodrama'; the small orchestra, eight players only, was dragged from the safe anonymity of the orchestra pit into the glare of the stage. A few years later appeared
227 *Oedipus Rex* (1927), a fusion of opera and oratorio sung in Latin, which perhaps owes something to Honegger's *King David* (1921) and can certainly trace an ancestry through such French mixed genres as Berlioz's *The Damnation of Faust* (described as a 'dramatic legend') and Félicien David's curious experiments to Montéclair's *Jephté* and the Italian dramatic oratorio.

When in 1951 he wrote an identifiable, full-length opera, *The*
228 *Rake's Progress*, he not only ignored the current techniques such as atonalism and serialism, but equally avoided the chromatic elaboration, the organic structural build-up into complete acts and the orchestral ascendancy that had been the nineteenth century's legacy. Instead, using his own particular brand of diatonicism, he wrote a 'number' opera, in which the arias were accompanied by the orchestra

227 An impressive scene from Stravinsky's oratorio-like opera, *Oedipus Rex*, in a 1965 Warsaw production by Konrad Swinarski, with decor by Jan Kosinski.

– eighteenth-century methods, reworked in the twentieth. This was in a way appropriate, for the libretto, by W.H. Auden and Chester Kallman (in Stravinsky's opinion one of the finest ever written) was inspired by William Hogarth's celebrated series of engravings published in 1735.

Stravinsky's works immediately following *The Rite of Spring* puzzled his audiences. They were anti-climactic; opulent, full-scale works were now being replaced by small-scale, spare works. Far from writing music to console or uplift us, he was misusing his talents on burlesques and fairy-tales. Moreover, his music was difficult, both to perform and to listen to. Meanwhile, in Germany in the period after the First World War a new generation of composers was arising whose works, while reflecting the disillusion and general *malaise* of the times, rejected the complications of conventional opera for a simpler approach. The stage works written by Bertolt Brecht and Kurt Weill (*The Threepenny Opera*, 1928; *The Rise and Fall of the City of* 229
*Mahogonny*, 1930) manifested a deliberately 'anti-operatic' style,

with popular elements from cabaret and the dance-hall replacing the rhetoric of Wagner and Strauss. When Hitler came to power Weill left Germany for the United States, where he achieved considerable success on Broadway as a writer of musicals. Another refugee was the Austrian Ernst Krenek, many of whose works, for example *Pallas Athene weint* (1955), are written in the twelve-note idiom, but who
230 first won fame with *Jonny spielt auf* ('Johnny Strikes up', 1927), which exploited, perhaps for the first time in opera, the jazz idiom which for some years had been invading Europe.

Another gifted composer who also had to leave Hitler's Germany was Paul Hindemith (1895–1963). His output includes a children's opera, *Wir bauen eine Stadt* ('We Build a City', 1931), an example that has been followed by numerous composers, including Aaron Copland and Benjamin Britten; the fine *Cardillac* (1926, revised 1952); and his masterpiece, *Mathis der Maler* (Zürich, 1938), the last opera that he wrote in Germany before he left for the United States. It revolves round its main character, the painter Matthias Grünewald, and debates the problems of the artist in society; the text is by Hindemith himself, and the conclusion which he draws, that the artist can best serve society by dedication to his art alone, is one that can hardly commend itself to totalitarian régimes of whatever persuasion.

228 (*left*) David Hockney's sets for *The Rake's Progress* (Glyndebourne, 1975) used the cross-hatching characteristic of Hogarth's engravings. Don Garrard (Trulove), Jill Gomez (Anne), Leo Goeke (Tom) and Donald Gramm (Nick Shadow).

229 Set by Caspar Neher (1897–1962) for Kurt Weill's *The Rise and Fall of the City of Mahagonny*, Leipzig, 1930.

230 A scene from Krenek's *Jonny spielt auf*, Leipzig, 1927.

Exactly contemporary with Hindemith was Carl Orff, who cultivated a deliberately simplistic style which he applied not only to folk or fairy tales such as *Der Mond* (1939) and *Die Bernauerin* (1947), but also to settings of Latin texts such as *Carmina Burana* (1937), and to Sophoclean tragedy (*Antigonae*, 1949).

The younger generation of German composers includes Giselher Klebe (b. 1925) and Hans Werner Henze (b. 1926). Klebe has some half-dozen operas to his credit, ranging from *Die Räuber*, based on Schiller, to Greek tragedy (*Alkmene*). Henze is the most outstanding German composer since the Second World War. His output includes

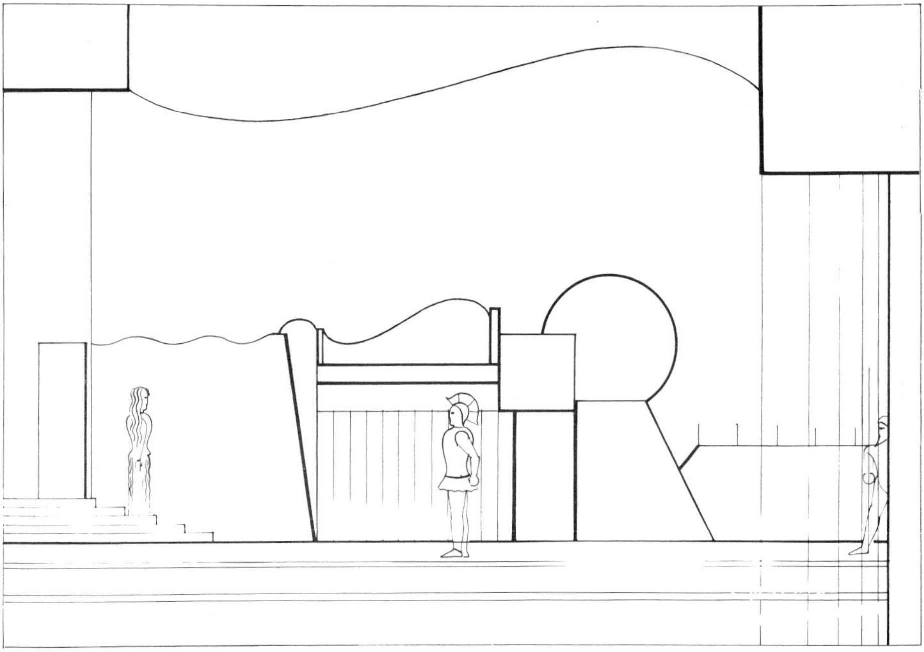

231 Design by Oskar Schlemmer (1888–1943) for Hindemith's *Mörder, Hoffnung der Frauen* (1921). Schlemmer was at one time head of the department of theatrical design at the Bauhaus.

radio operas (*Ein Landarzt*, *Das Ende einer Welt*); a school opera (*Moralities*, workings by W.H. Auden of some fables by Aesop, first produced in Cincinnati); a reworking of the Manon story, *Boulevard Solitude*; a comic opera, *Der junge Lord*. Like many writers today, he is concerned with responsibility, with the relationship of men and
233 women to each other. *Elegy for Young Lovers*, like Hindemith's *Mathis der Maler*, deals with the artist in relation to society, a relationship which Henze seemed to find increasingly difficult himself. In the late 1960s he moved sharply to the political left, which was naturally reflected in his subsequent works for the stage: while *El Cimarrón* (1970), *La Cubana* (1975), *We Come to the River* (1976) and *The English Cat* (1983) – the last two to librettos by the British playwright Edward Bond – may deal with Western imperialism and the class war, the fertile exuberance of Henze's musical invention has remained intact.

Karlheinz Stockhausen (b. 1928) turned to the stage comparatively late in his composing life with a planned cycle of seven operas, one for each day of the week – thus outdoing Wagner. Largely autobiographical in inspiration, the first two 'days', *Donnerstag* (1981) and *Samstag* (1984), have used dance, speech, song, massed choruses and instrumental groups on stage to match if not surpass the Wagnerian *Gesamtkunstwerk*, and the admixture of pre-recorded tape and electronic enhancement of vocal and instrumental lines during performance has significantly extended the frontiers of opera's traditional sound-world.

Rather more traditional in respect of forces used, though scarcely less challenging, have been the operas of Aribert Reimann (b. 1936): his *Lear*, written for Dietrich Fischer-Dieskau, has been successfully staged on both sides of the Atlantic.

The 'new look' in opera came to Italy rather slowly. In Giacomo Puccini (1858–1924) Verdi found a successor, less of a genius no doubt, but with the same eye for the 'human' situation and the same mistrust of the mystical or the metaphysical. *La Bohème* (1896) and *Tosca* 234, 235

232 A set by Helmut Jürgens for the 1948 Munich revival of Carl Orff's *Die Kluge* ('The Wise Girl').

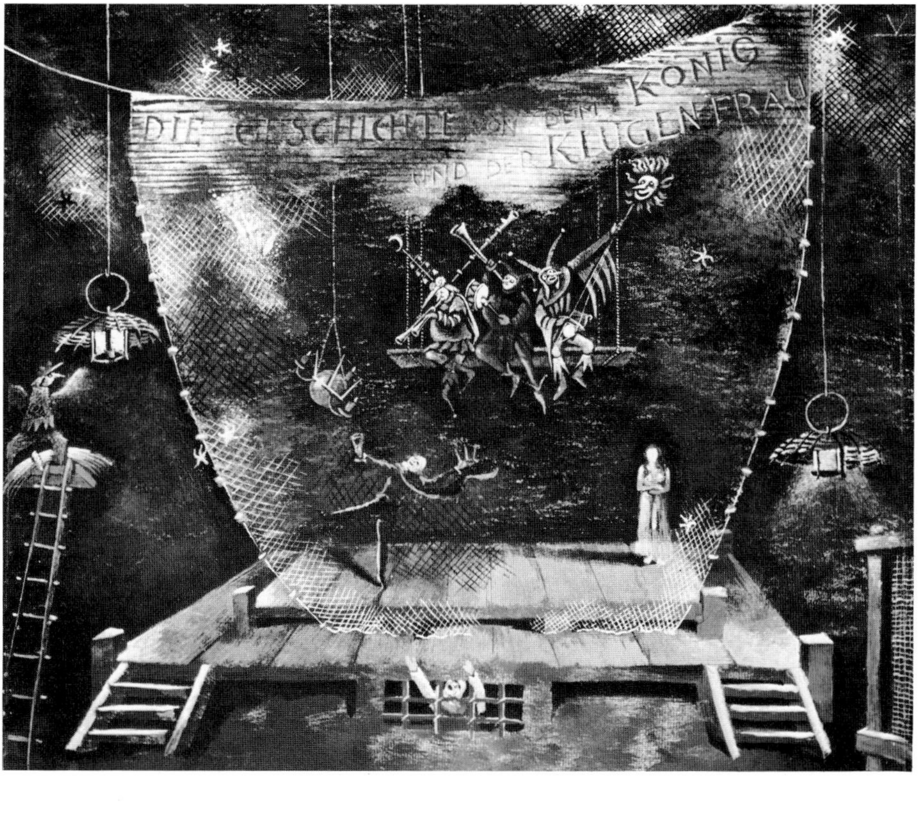

233 Dietrich Fischer-Dieskau as the Poet in Hans Werner Henze's *Elegy for Young Lovers*, Schwetzingen, 1961.

(1900), both examples of the *verismo* or realist school, show him as a mature artist, fully in command of his resources, as much at home in the violence of Sardou's melodrama as in the impecunious *bonhomie* of Murger's Left Bank Paris (one is reminded of the genre paintings, pathetic and sentimental, so popular at the time). In the exquisite
237, 239 *Madama Butterfly* (1904) Puccini explored the vein of exotic, Orient-based operas opened up by Bizet and Delibes, while his brilliantly successful *Gianni Schicchi* (1918), one of a triptych of one-act operas, showed that his instinct for passionate melodrama did not preclude a
236 flair for comedy. His operatic 'Western', *La fanciulla del West* (1910), has recently gained steadily in popularity, and the discovery in 1982 of
238, 250 Alfano's original completion of the unfinished *Turandot*, suppressed by Toscanini in 1926, has added to rather than solved the problems surrounding Puccini's most ambitious and challenging opera.

Puccini and his contemporaries Mascagni (*Cavalleria Rusticana*, 1890), Leoncavallo (*I Pagliacci*, 1892), Giordano (*Andrea Chénier*, 1896) and Cilea (*Adriana Lecouvreur*, 1902) made few concessions to the 'progressive' music of their day. But later composers such as
240, 242 Respighi, Pizzetti and Malipiero could hardly avoid some influence

from Wagner's theories, and such works as *La Nave* and *La Figlia di Jorio* (Pizzetti, both to words by d'Annunzio) or Respighi's *La Fiamma* aim at 'music drama' rather than 'opera'. Since the Second World War musical Italy has experienced almost a second Renaissance, and in opera there has been a willingness to experiment that is a refreshing contrast to the conservatism of the nineteenth century. Three outstanding names in contemporary Italy are Luigi Dallapiccola (1904–75), Luigi Nono (b. 1924) and Luciano Berio (b. 1925); each has made contributions to the theatre, and Dallapiccola's *Il Prigionero* (1950) has become accepted as a classic of our time. Berio's *La Vera Storia* (a twentieth re-telling of *Il Trovatore*) was premiered at La Scala in 1982, and *Un Re in Ascolto* at Salzburg in 1984.

Two of the most delightful small-scale operas of this century come from France – Ravel's *L'Heure espagnole* (1911) and *L'Enfant et les Sortilèges* (1925). Poulenc's *Les Mamelles de Tirésias* and Milhaud's *Le Pauvre Matelot* are similar but lighter in style. Milhaud has also composed essays in the grand manner, such as *Christophe Colomb* (1930), *Bolivar* (1943) and *David* (1954). The works of Arthur Honegger (Swiss by parentage, French by adoption) show a very

234 Puccini's *La Bohème* in Paris, 1898: Schaunard (M. Fugère), Marcel (M. Bouvet), Rodolph (M. Maréchal) and Colline (M. Isnardon).

235 (*left*) Ljuba Welitsch as Tosca, in Puccini's opera.

236 (*below*) Enrico Caruso as Johnson and Emmy Destinn as 'the Girl' in the first performance of Puccini's *The Girl of the Golden West*, Metropolitan, New York, 1910.

237 (*right*) Geraldine Farrar as Cio-Cio-San in Puccini's *Madama Butterfly*.

238 (*far right*) Eva Turner, considered by Franco Alfano, the Italian composer who completed Puccini's unfinished *Turandot*, as the ideal Turandot.

239 (*below, right*) Victoria de los Angeles as Cio-Cio-San, and John Lanigan as Pinkerton, in a production of *Madama Butterfly* at Covent Garden, 1957.

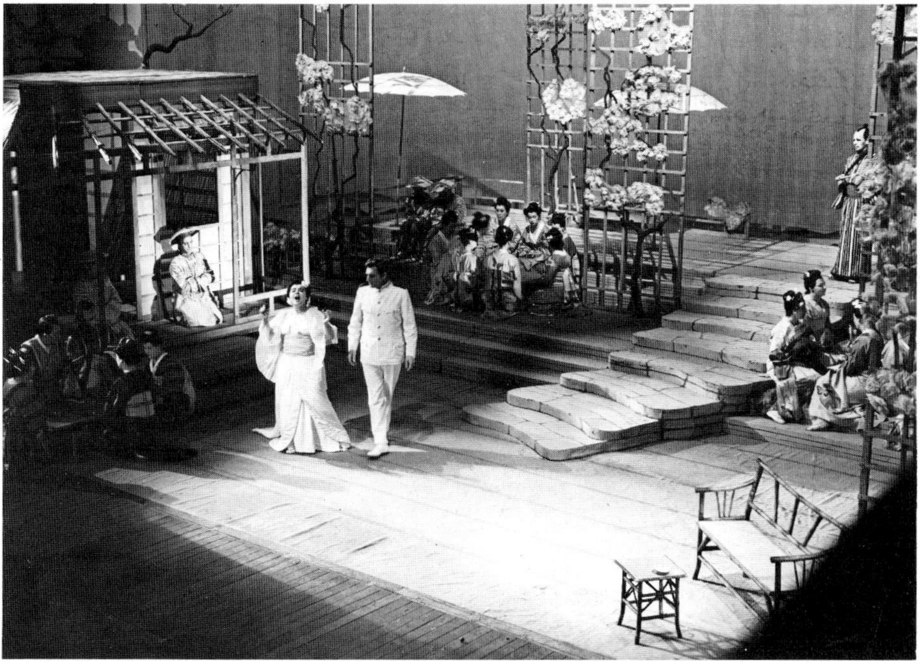

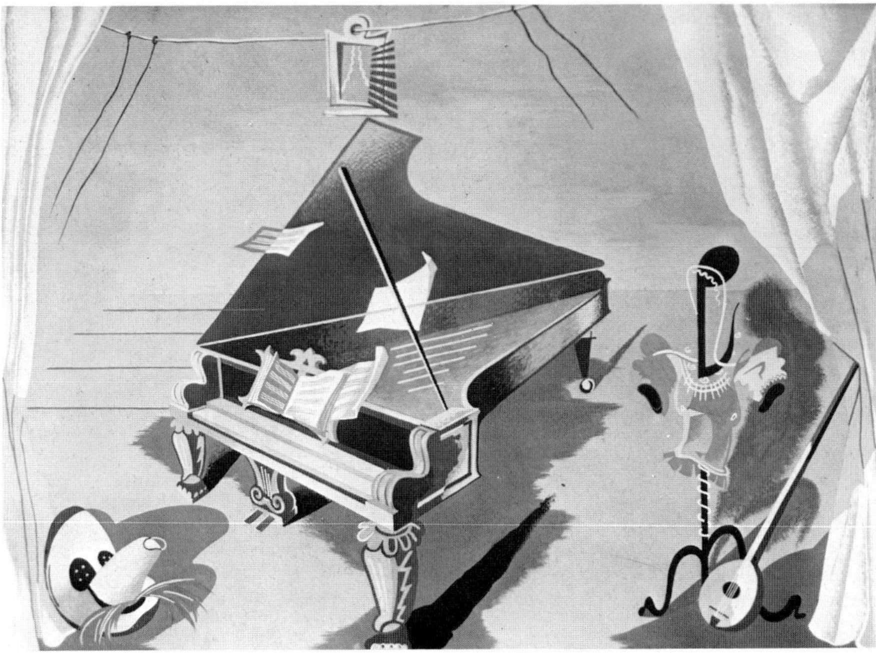

varied approach; perhaps the most notable are the two opera-oratorios, *Le Roi David* and *Jeanne d'Arc au Bûcher* (1936). The post-war French opera most likely to retain world-wide acceptance is Poulenc's *Dialogues des Carmélites* (1957); this harrowing account of the fate of a group of nuns in the French Revolution has a relevance far beyond mere time and place.

In Russia interest in opera has been intensified since the Revolution and particularly since 1945, with new opera houses erected in all the important centres. The repertory embraces the accepted classics of Western music, with substantial contributions by Soviet composers such as Shaporin, Kabalevsky, Dzerzhinsky, Reinhold Glière, Khrennikov, Spadavecchia and many others.

The substance and form of Soviet opera have been a constant preoccupation of composers and theorists. Opera has in the past tended to be selective rather than universal in its appeal, and early Soviet operas, such as Pashchenko's *The Revolt of the Eagles* or Zolatoryov's *The Decembrists*, were criticized because the music was insufficiently strong to represent the subject. But we also find Prokofiev being reproached for 'formalism', while Shostakovich's

240 (*left*) Curtain design by Enrico Prampolini (a former member of the Italian Futurist movement, which began in 1909) for Gian Francesco Malipiero's *I capricci di Callot*, Rome, 1942.

241 (*right*) Erté's attractive set for Poulenc's *Les Mamelles de Tirésias*, Opéra-Comique, Paris, 1947.

242 (*below*) Pizzetti's *Murder in the Cathedral*, Sadler's Wells Opera, 1958.

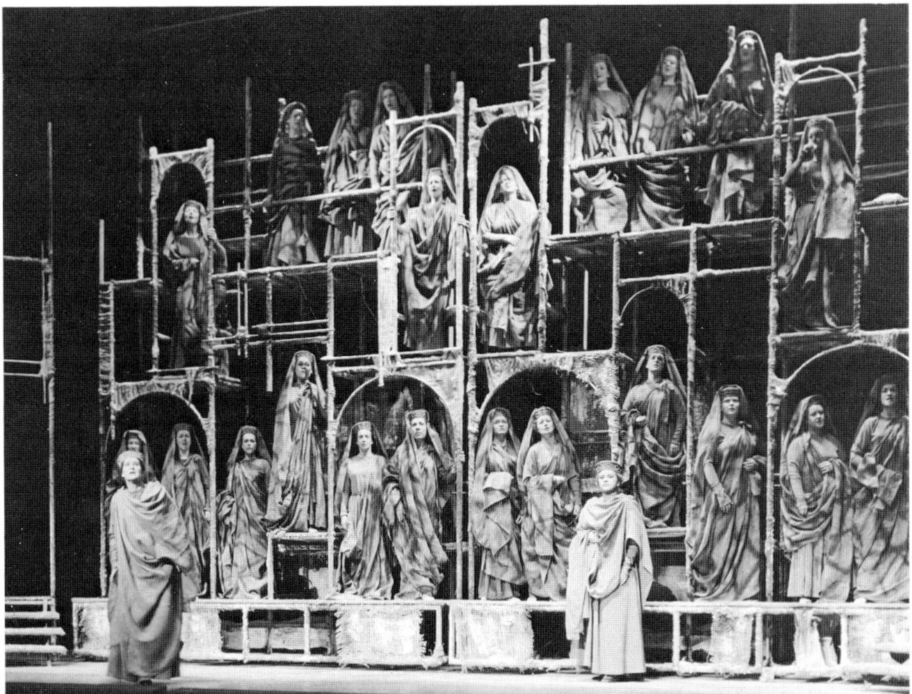

*The Nose* (1930, based on Gogol) was subjected to official disapproval by reason of 'eccentric effects, of the onomatopoeic kind'. The most notorious case of official reproof, in this instance a *volte face* after initial acclamation, was that of Shostakovich's *The Lady Macbeth of the Mtsensk District* (1934). The article in *Pravda* of 28 January 1936 condemning the work made much of the violence and discordance of the music and the lack of simple, comprehensible melody. The opera remained in disgrace until revised, as *Katerina Ismailova*, in 1963, but outside the USSR the original version has enjoyed wide currency on stage and has been successfully recorded.

In the 1930s there was an attempt to solve, or rather evade, the problem by harnessing popular song to the needs of the stage, as in Dzerzhinsky's *The Quiet Don*, based on Sholokhov's novel, Zhelobinsky's *The Kamarinsky Peasant* and Khrennikov's *In the Storm*. Another solution was to simplify and countrify the plots, to a formula that had worked brilliantly in Smetana's *The Bartered Bride*. An example is *Daisi* ('Twilight', 1923), by the Georgian composer Paliashvili. This is a tale of true, peasant love trampled on by ruthless feudalism. The setting, a festival lasting the whole night long, offers the excuse for song, dance and spectacle on the lines of Borodin's *Prince Igor*, and the music mingles genuine Georgian folk-tunes with the composer's own folk-like melody.

Folk song and folklore generally, the art of the people, has understandably acquired an almost mystical significance, and is being studied intensively, especially in the more distant provinces. Georgia, in the Caucasus, has a lively folk tradition, and a musical and theatrical heritage that antedates the Revolution. The folk music of Azerbaidjan, east of Georgia and bordering the Caspian Sea, betrays similarities to Arab music (Iran lies immediately to the south). The main musical form, the *mugam*, is an improvised rhapsody not unlike the Indian *raga*, and the local instruments include some on which intervals of less than a semitone can be played. *Leili i Medzhun*, the first Azerbaidjan opera, written in 1907 by Uzir Gadzhibekov, makes use of these local instruments and also demands vocal extemporization in the traditional style. Neither this nor operas from provinces even further afield, such as Tashkent, have yet been produced in the West, but one cannot help feeling that it is from these remoter centres that the most vital Soviet operas will eventually come.

As it is, the Western world's first-hand knowledge of Soviet opera

243 Dzerzhinsky's *Tikkhy Don* ('The Quiet Don') at the Kirov theatre, Leningrad, 1935.

is confined to the work of those composers with an international reputation in other forms. Of these the most accomplished technically is Prokofiev (1891–1953); such works as *The Love for Three Oranges* *191*
(1921), *The Fiery Angel* (1927, but not produced until 1955) and *The Gambler* (1929) reveal both his genius and limitations, and his epic *War and Peace* (1946) has proved very popular in the West.

England in the twentieth century has become an exporter as well as an importer of opera, though the trade balance is still unfavourable. This development began as early as 1906, when Leipzig mounted *The Wreckers*, by Ethel Smyth. Berlin followed suit the next year, with Delius's *A Village Romeo and Juliet*. Both works were subsequently mounted in London by Sir Thomas Beecham, whose own opera company and its successor, the British National Opera Company, gave the standard repertory in English and also encouraged native composers such as Vaughan Williams and Gustav Holst. The former's *Hugh the Drover*, long in the repertory of the Sadler's Wells company, was a rather obvious essay in the folk-song style; Holst's one-act opera, *The Perfect Fool*, parodying grand-opera conventions, and his chamber opera *Sāvitri* revealed a decidedly interesting and individual personality.

244 A new era opened on 7 June 1945, when Benjamin Britten's *Peter Grimes* was first given at Sadler's Wells theatre. This work, speaking a language at once national, international and personal, thrust itself confidently into the centre of the operatic world and was hailed for what it is, a masterpiece. Moreover, it was no flash in the pan, for Britten followed it with a series of new works, greatly diversified in subject-matter and form, but all shot through with his unmistakable
246 personality. Large-scale works (*Billy Budd*, *A Midsummer Night's Dream*), chamber operas (*The Rape of Lucretia*, *The Turn of the Screw*) or children's operas (*Noye's Fludde*), all reveal an equally secure touch. The latter, a modern 'liturgical' drama intended for performance in
245 church, was followed by three more church operas (*Curlew River*, *The Burning Fiery Furnace*, *The Prodigal Son*). In these works – part pageant, part opera, part worship – Britten, like so many other artists of the present-day theatre, sought to widen the area of dramatic experience beyond the four walls, proscenium arch and fixed stage of the traditional theatre. His last opera, *Death in Venice*, was first performed in 1973, three years before his death.

Britten, though the most prolific of modern British opera composers, was far from alone. Michael Tippett was born in 1905, eight years before Britten. In his four operas *The Midsummer Marriage* (1955), *King Priam* (1962), *The Knot Garden* (1970) and *The Ice Break* (1976) he clothes his own recondite libretti with music of great individuality. The younger generation of British composers whose works have reached a public beyond the UK include Thea Musgrave (*Mary, Queen of Scots*, 1976; *Harriet, the Woman Called Moses*, 1985), Alexander Goehr (*Arden Must Die*, 1966; *Behold the Sun*, 1985), Harrison Birtwistle (*Punch and Judy*, 1968; *The Mask of Orpheus*, 1986), Peter Maxwell Davies (*Taverner*, 1972; *The Lighthouse*, 1980), Nicholas Maw (*The Rising of the Moon*, 1970) and Stephen Oliver (*Tom Jones*, 1976; *The Duchess of Malfi*, 1979).

In the United States the post-Menotti/Barber generation has tended to play safe by using established novels and plays as sources for new operas (Thomas Pasatieri's *The Seagull* and *Washington Square*; Carlisle Floyd's *Of Mice and Men*; Stephen Paulus's *The Postman*

244, 245, 246 *Left*: Benjamin Britten at rehearsal. *Right*: Peter Pears in Britten's *Curlew River*, 1964. *Below*: A stunning evocation of the moonlit forest, with Tytania (Elizabeth Gale) asleep, in Britten's *A Midsummer Night's Dream* (Glyndebourne, 1984). Staging by Peter Hall, revived by Michael McCaffery, designed by John Bury.

*Always Rings Twice*). But the 'minimalist' composer Philip Glass is thoroughly uncompromising in his choice of subject matter: *Einstein on the Beach* (1976, dealing with the physicist), *Satyagraha* (1980, Gandhi's philosophy of non-violent resistance, sung in Sanskrit) and *Akhnaten* (1984, a study of the monotheist Egyptian Pharaoh) all deal with individuals who have changed the world. Glass's music consists mostly of slowly evolving ostinatos of the simplest melodic and harmonic patterns, which are either literally 'entrancing' or absolutely infuriating, according to taste. His operas have proved highly popular with an entirely new audience. Composers of more mainstream works are John Eaton, whose *The Tempest* (1985) has been judged one of the most ambitious and successful of new American operas, and Dominick Argento, some of whose earlier works have been heard in Europe (*A Postcard from Morocco*, 1971; *The Voyage of Edgar Allan Poe*, 1976; *Casanova's Homecoming*, 1985).

The widening of opera's horizons has been given a new dimension through modern technology, which has presented us with some unique problems and opportunities. First came the invention of the gramophone, which in its early days took the 'golden voices' of Caruso, Melba and others into the homes of people who could never have heard these singers in the flesh. Nowadays long-playing records, compact discs, cassettes and modern stereophonic recording techniques have brought the sound spectrum to an almost damaging degree of perfection – a perfection unattainable in live performance – and we can study operatic masterpieces at home in a fashion previously undreamed of.

Film made its biggest impact on opera when the addition of the sound track made possible the transmutation of opera into film: *Carmen* (Francesco Rosi), *Don Giovanni* (Joseph Losey), *La Traviata* Zeffirelli), *Boris Godunov*, *Der Rosenkavalier* and *Fidelio* are among the operas that have been so treated. In some cases, one might say, ill-treated, for some of the adaptations will hardly serve. It is not enough simply to film a staged opera, but on the other hand elaborate scenes 'on location' are risky. They seldom ring true.

So far few operas have been written specifically for the cinema (an interesting experiment was the French *Les Parapluies de Cherbourg*, directed by Jacques Demy, with music by Michel Legrand, 1963), and it seems that as yet no one has fully exploited the resources that are peculiar to film. Modern camera techniques make possible illusions

247 Michael Tippett's first opera, *The Midsummer Marriage*, first performed in 1955 at Covent Garden, with sets designed by Barbara Hepworth.

and magical transformations of all kinds that not only make the average theatrical devices look intolerably clumsy but, what is more important, offer a totally new range of visual beauty. This, in conjunction with the use of tapes and electronic music, opens up the possibility of a new audio-visual art.

Radio, like the gramophone, suffers from the disability of being one-dimensional; nevertheless, radio operas have been written, for example, Menotti's *The Old Maid and the Thief*. But the lack of the visual element is a serious handicap, and whatever radio opera is, it is not genuine 'opera'. Television opera is in a rather different category. Here one drawback is the small screen, but one does at least see something, though the ear may be assaulted by the poor quality of sound reproduction that most commercial sets give us. The best-known television operas are Menotti's *Amahl and the Night Visitors* (1951) and Britten's *Owen Wingrave* (1971), though both have been transferred easily to the stage. The wide currency of video cassettes has added a visual equivalent to the gramophone: recordings of opera-house productions can now be studied and enjoyed in the living room.

Finally, there is the whole new range of sounds made possible by

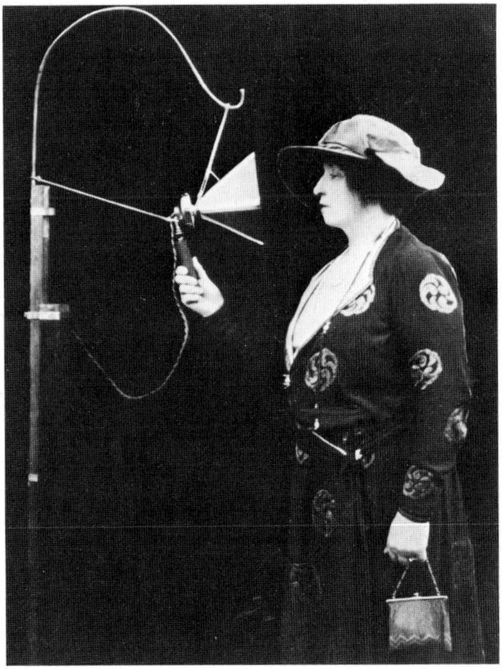

248 Dame Nellie Melba (1861–1931), the first of the line of great singers to come from Australia. She is seen here broadcasting a song recital from the Marconi works at Chelmsford, Essex, in 1920 – two years before the British Broadcasting Company (the forerunner of the present British Broadcasting Corporation) came into being. This was one of the very first international broadcasts.

electronics and the tape recorder. Already in 1959 these novel effects had been combined with more conventional music in Karl-Birger 249 Blomdahl's space opera, *Aniara*, produced in Stockholm. Since then there have appeared a number of operas that include this synthetic taped music, as for instance *Dreaming about Therese* (1965), by another Swedish composer, Lars Johan Werle, Nono's *Intolleranza*, and Birtwistle's *The Mask of Orpheus*.

These typically twentieth-century techniques have given additional meaning to the concept of 'total theatre'. The term, associated with the French producer and choreographer Maurice Béjart, is much in the minds of today's composers. The Czech composer Vaclav Kaslik, who produced Nono's *Intolleranza* at Venice in 1961, sees the future music theatre as a synthesis of sung and spoken words, acting and dance, as in the best contemporary musicals. The idea is carried still further by such works as *Labyrint*, by the Dutch composer Peter Schat, produced in 1966 at the Holland Festival, and Bernd Alois Zimmermann's *Die Soldaten*, first performed at Cologne (the city which commissioned the work) in 1965 – 'a pan-acoustical form of music theatre, which fuses together every element of speech, song,

249 The final scene of Karl-Birger Blomdahl's *Aniara*, with decor by Sven Erixon, Stockholm, 1959.

music, painting, film, ballet, pantomime, tape montage'.

In an enterprise of this complexity the producer is paramount, the composer no more than *primus inter pares*. The composer first yielded his authority to the conductor, as Verdi during most of his life, and Wagner during his last years, were glad to do. The producer began to enter the scene at about the turn of the century. This development can be traced directly to the Duke of Meiningen's theatrical company. It brought a new conception of unity into whatever happened on the stage, whether it was the movement of individual actors, the handling of crowds or the control of decor and lighting. This, in the period 1874–90, had influence as far afield as Paris and Moscow, with far-reaching effects on Stanislavsky and his one-time pupil, Meyerhold. Stanislavsky followed the Meiningen theory of naturalism and realism, in both acting and decor, but by about 1905 Meyerhold had advanced beyond this point of view and was veering towards the theories of such writers as Georg Fuchs, of Munich, who in his *Die Schaubühne der Zukunft* was advocating a deliberate move away from the 'literary' play, towards a 'total' theatre, visually orientated, drawing inspiration from both the ballet and the circus, with gesture and movements in harmony with the decor and, where music is added, in close agreement with that. The operas which Meyerhold produced included *Boris Godunov* (with Chaliapin), and Gluck's *Orfeo*; he also produced a *Tristan und Isolde*, in 1909, of which he said, 'the opera should be a sort of pantomime', and he criticized the singers for moving in response not to the music, but to the libretto.

It was at about this time that Max Reinhardt began his career as a producer, and soon became noted for his imaginative handling of big crowd scenes, especially in the open air, as in the play *Jedermann* (at Salzburg) or in large arenas like Olympia in London. Also at this time there took place the first experiments in the use of Roman arenas for large-scale open-air opera, as for example at Orange, or at Béziers in south-west France, where Fauré's *Prométhée* was staged in 1900 – performances that were the prototypes of the more ambitious productions, aided by the technological expertise derived from the
*251* cinema, that are now a regular feature at Verona, Trieste, Rome (Caracalla Baths), on the lake at Bregenz and elsewhere.

Reinhardt was the father-figure of German producers; one of his pupils was Carl Ebert, who with the conductor Fritz Busch set new standards of opera production in England at Glyndebourne. Other influential German-speaking producers include Rudolf Hartmann, Günther Rennert, Otto Schenk and Walter Felsenstein (1901–75), whose directorship of the Komische Oper in East Berlin gave birth to the social-realist school of opera production; among his pupils are Götz Friedrich, Joachim Herz and Harry Kupfer, whose work tends towards the socio-analytical at the expense of the merely picturesque. Wieland Wagner's productions of his grandfather's works at Bayreuth caused much controversy in the 1950s, but, in departing from the letter if not the spirit of Richard Wagner's wishes, he had been anticipated by Wagner productions in many other German cities. The extreme abstraction of his method was for a time much imitated, but after his death in 1966 there was a return to colourful pictorialism, albeit crossed with social analysis, with Patrice Chéreau's centenary
*253* staging of *Der Ring des Nibelungen* at Bayreuth in 1976. Not all that is important in opera production, however, is confined to Germany: Chéreau is active in France, and Giorgio Strehler's work is seen far too seldom outside Italy.

Modern scenographers are less interested in fashioning a more or less realistic set, with costumes to match, than in creating a visual

250 A spectacular staging of Puccini's *Turandot* on the floating stage on Lake Constance at Bregenz.

251 A floodlit performance of Mascagni's *Cavalleria Rusticana* in the great Roman Amphitheatre at Verona.

252 The breathtaking, multi-million-pound new Opera House at Sydney. Begun in 1959, it opened in 1973.

framework suited to the emotional and musical needs of the drama. They work in three dimensions, with actions taking place on various levels, and with colour and lighting as the most important ingredients. Alfred Roller, working with Mahler in Vienna, was an early disciple of Appia; by his time all stages were lit with electricity, and it was possible for Roller to put into practice Appia's theories as to the use of light as a dynamic dramatic agent. Scenographers who have made significant contributions to this aspect of opera production in Europe include Caspar Neher (also a librettist), Hans Strohbach, Josef Svoboda and Ralph Koltai. Luchino Visconti and his pupil Franco
50 Zeffirelli, who both came to opera via the cinema, favour a more representational, spectacular style of design, and since the war there has been a move towards using painters as set designers, with varying degrees of success – they have included Oskar Kokoschka, Marc
104, 228 Chagall, John Piper, Sidney Nolan and David Hockney. Identifiable schools of design have been associated with many of those named, yet none has remained on top for long: the 1983 decor for the *Ring* at Bayreuth (William Dudley) sought to re-create a visual realism not all that far removed from Wagner's own.

Many of those mentioned made their reputation in the realms of spoken drama or the cinema. The old gibe against opera, that what was too silly to be said could be sung, was itself too foolish to be considered as an aesthetic criticism. Its rationalistic approach missed the whole point of opera. It is therefore encouraging to have seen such alert men of the theatre as Jean-Louis Barrault, John Gielgud, Peter Hall and Jonathan Miller bringing their creative minds to the opera house. It is true that opera production has its own pitfalls, and the solutions adopted by, for example, Peter Brook at Covent Garden during the 1940s did not always commend themselves to musicians; more recently Brook has turned to drastically adapting existing works to his own particular needs (*Le Tragédie de Carmen*, 1981). But, as we have frequently stressed, music is only a part of opera; it does, however, add a new dimension to theatrical experience, and in so doing creates a new art form with its own peculiar limitations and opportunities. If this is acknowledged nothing but good can come of the transfusion of new blood from outside the narrow confines of the opera house.

In any case, the confines have already widened. A significant feature of today's art world is the blurring of the lines of demarcation

253 In Patrice Chéreau's influential 1976 production of Wagner's *Ring*, the Rhine was represented not by flowing water but by a dam. Scene 1 of *Das Rheingold*, with Zoltan Kelemen as Alberich.

between art forms, and opera by its very nature is a suitable field for such experimentation. It is essentially a mixed form, and there is a constantly fluctuating balance of forces between librettist, composer, designer, producer and audience. Some of the apparently disruptive elements of work today, which seem to challenge opera's most cherished conventions, from the art of singing to the validity of the opera house itself as a building, are in fact less symbols of decay than reassuring evidence that opera, far from being moribund, is as vital today as it has ever been.

# Select Bibliography


GENERAL WORKS OF REFERENCE

*The New Grove Dictionary of Music and Musicians*, edited by Stanley Sadie (20 vols, London, 1980)

*Musik in Geschichte und Gegenwart* (14 vols, Kassel and Basle, 1949–68)

*Enciclopedia dello Spettacolo* (10 vols, Rome, 1951–66; profusely illustrated)

*The Oxford Companion to the Theatre* (London, 1951)

Dubech, Lucien, *Histoire générale illustrée du théâtre* (5 vols, Paris, 1931–4)

Gascoigne, Bamber, *World Theatre: an Illustrated History* (London, 1966)

Gregor, Joseph, *The Russian Theatre* (London, 1930)

GENERAL HISTORIES OF OPERA

Drummond, John D., *Opera in Perspective* (London, 1980)

Grout, Donald J., *A Short History of Opera* (1st ed., 2 vols, New York and London, 1947; 2nd rev. ed., 1 vol., 1965)

Loewenberg, Alfred, *Annals of Opera* (1st ed., Cambridge, 1943; 3rd rev. ed., 1978)

Rosenthal, Harold, and John Warrack, *Concise Oxford Dictionary of Opera* (2nd ed., Oxford, 1979)

OPERA SYNOPSES

Kobbé Gustav, *The Complete Opera Book*. New edition revised by the Earl of Harewood (London, 1979)

Lubbock, Mark, *The Complete Book of Light Opera* (London, 1962)

Newman, Ernest, *Opera Nights* (London, 1943)

Newman, Ernest, *More Opera Nights* (London, 1954)

Newman, Ernest, *Wagner Nights* (London, 1949)

BOOKS ON INDIVIDUAL COMPOSERS

*Vincenzo Bellini, His Life and Operas*, Herbert Weinstock (London, 1972)

*Bizet*, Winton Dean (2nd ed., London, 1975)

*The Music of Benjamin Britten*, Peter Evans (London, 1970)

*Donizetti and His Operas*, William Ashbrook (Cambridge, 1982)

*Gluck*, Alfred Einstein (2nd ed., London, 1964)

*Handel and the Opera Seria*, Winton Dean (London, 1970)

*Leoš Janáček, a Biography*, Jaroslav Vogel (London, 1981)

*Monteverdi*, Denis Arnold (London, 1963)

*The Operas of Mozart*, William Mann (London, 1977)

*Jacques Offenbach*, Alexander Faris (London, 1980)

*Puccini*, Mosco Carner (2nd ed., London, 1974)

*Purcell*, J.A. Westrup (2nd ed., London, 1965)

*Rameau*, Cuthbert Girdlestone (London, 1957; rev. ed., paperback, 1969)

*Rossini*, Richard Osborne (London, 1986)

*Strauss: A Critical Study of the Operas*, William Mann (London, 1964)

*Arthur Sullivan, A Victorian Musician*, Arthur Jacobs (London, 1984)

*The Man Verdi*, Frank Walker (London, 1962)

*The Operas of Verdi*, Julian Budden (3 vols, London, 1970–81)

*The Life of Richard Wagner*, Ernest Newman (4 vols, London, 1933–47; paperback, Cambridge, 1976)

*Wagner*, Barry Millington (London, 1984)

*Wagner's 'Ring' and its Symbols*, Robert Donington (London, 1963)

*Weber*, John Warrack (2nd ed., Cambridge, 1976)

BOOKS DEALING WITH PARTICULAR ASPECTS OF OPERA

Bornoff, Jack, *Music Theatre in a Changing Society* (UNESCO, 1968)

Chase, Gilbert, *The Music of Spain* (2nd rev. ed., paperback, New York, 1959)

Demuth, Norman, *French Opera. Its Development to the Revolution* (Horsham, 1963)

Dent, Edward J., *Foundations of English Opera. A Study of Musical Drama in England during the Seventeenth Century* (Cambridge, 1928; 2nd ed., New York, 1965)

Dent, Edward J., *The Rise of Romantic Opera* (ed. Winton Dean, Cambridge, 1976)

Engel, Lehman, *The American Musical Theater: A Consideration* (CBS Records, 1967)

Gatti, Carlo, *Il Teatro all Scala* (2 vols, Milan, 1964)

Genest, Emile, *L'Opéra-comique connu et inconnu* (Paris, 1925)

Henderson, W.J., *Some Forerunners of Italian Opera* (London, 1911)

Hughes, Spike, *Glyndebourne: A History of the Festival Opera* (2nd ed., Newton Abbot, 1981)

Kerman, Joseph, *Opera as Drama* (New York, 1952)

Krause, Ernst, *Die grossen Opernbühnen Europas* (Kassel, 1968)

Merkling, Frank, John W. Freeman, and Gerald Fitzgerald, *The Golden Horseshoe* (New York and London, 1965). An account of the Metropolitan Opera, New York

Newman, Ernest, *Gluck and the Opera* (London, 1895; reprinted 1964)

Prawy, Marcel, *The Vienna Opera* (Eng. ed., London, 1970)

Robinson, Michael F., *Opera before Mozart* (London, 1966)

Rosenthal, Harold, *Two Centuries of Opera at Covent Garden* (London, 1958)

Rosselli, John, *The Opera Industry in Italy from Cimarosa to Verdi* (Cambridge, 1984)

Smith, Patrick J., *The Tenth Muse: A Historical Study of the Opera Libretto* (London, 1971)

Stuckenschmidt, H.H., *40 Jahre Oper* (Velber, near Hanover, 1964)

Traubner, Richard, *Operetta: A Theatrical History* (London, 1984)

White, Eric Walter, *A History of English Opera* (London, 1983)

White, Eric Walter, *The Rise of English Opera* (London, 1951)

Worsthorne, Simon Towneley, *Venetian Opera in the Seventeenth Century* (London, 1954)


# Sources of the Illustrations

*Sources not given in the following list will be found in the Photographic Acknowledgments, on page 247.*

1 Pen and wash drawing by Carlo Fontana from *Teatro di Tor di Nona del C. Carlo Fontana*. Trustees of Sir John Soane's Museum, London.

2 Engraving from Francesco Milizia, *Trattato Completo . . . del Teatro*, 1794. British Museum.

3 Courtesy Mrs Walter Gropius.

4 From *The Fleury Playbook*. MS, thirteenth century. Bibliothèque de la Ville, Orleans, MS 201, p. 230.

5 Intarsia wood panel attributed to Lorenzo Lotto, fifteenth century. Choir of Sta Maria Maggiore, Bergamo.

6 Miniature from a MS, fourteenth or fifteenth century, Bodleian Library, Oxford, MS Bodl. 264.

7 Medallion by Pisanello, *c.* 1446. British Museum.

8 Contemporary engraving by Jacques Callot.

9 Contemporary engraving by Remigio Cartagallina after Giulio Parigi. Uffizi, Florence.

10 Contemporary engraving by Carracius after Bernardo Buontalenti. Victoria and Albert Museum, London, Print Room.

11 Engraving by Barberis, nineteenth century. Raccolta Achille Bertarelli, Milan.

12 Engraving from A. Ademollo, *La Bell'Adriana a Milano*, 1628 (facsimile). British Museum.

13 Score of Monteverdi, *Orfeo*, 1615 (facsimile). Bibliotèque et Musée de l'Opéra, Paris.

14 Contemporary engraving. Raccolta Achille Bertarelli, Milan.

15 Engraving, eighteenth century. Museo Correr, Venice.

18, 19 Engravings by Alfonso Parigi, 1620. Raccolta Achille Bertarelli, Milan.

20 Nicola Sabbatini, *Practica di Fabricar Scene e Machine ne' Teatri*, 1638.
21 'La Décoration du Palais d'Apolon.' Engraving by Pierre Aveline after Giacomo Torelli, ?1683. Victoria and Albert Museum, London, Print Room.
22, 23 Pen and wash drawings, Bibliothèque et Musée de l'Opéra, Paris.
24 Contemporary engraving by Jacques Patin.
25 Painting by Paul Mignard, second half of seventeenth century. Musée Condé, Chantilly.
26 Engraving by Israel Silvestre, 1662. Musée de Versailles.
27 Engraving by Jean le Pautre from *Les Divertissements de Versailles*, 1676. Bibliothèque Nationale, Paris.
28 Title-page of Lully, *Armide*. Engraving by J. Dolivar after Jean Bérain, 1686. Raymond Mander and Joe Mitchenson Theatre Collection, London.
29 Pen and watercolour by Charles-Nicolas Cochin. Theatermuseum, Munich.
30 Watercolour attributed to Jean Bérain. Victoria and Albert Museum, London, Print Room.
31 Pen drawing by Giovanni Servandoni. National Museum, Stockholm.
32 Contemporary engraving by F. Chaveau after Carlo Vigarani. Bibliothèque et Musée de l'Opéra, Paris.
33 Contemporary engraving by Charles-Nicolas Cochin. Museo Teatrale alla Scala, Milan.
34 Engraving, seventeenth century.
35 Watercolour, 1786. Musée Carnavalet, Paris.
36 Engraving by François Poilly after Bonnat, early eighteenth century. Biblothèque de l'Arsenal, Paris.
37 Engraving after Forbet l'Ainé, 1623. Bibliothèque de l'Arsenal, Paris.
38 Design for Desbuches and Lamothe, *Issé*. Painting by François Boucher, 1742. Musée d'Amiens.
39 Costume design for M. Jelliote in Gossec, *Philémon et Baucis*. Pen and watercolour by Louis René Boquet. Victoria and Albert Museum, London, Print Room.
40 Pen and wash drawing by Inigo Jones. Devonshire Collection, Chatsworth. Reproduced by permission of the Trustees of the Chatsworth Settlement.
41 Title-page of Lawes, *Comus*, 1637.
42 'View of Rhodes', design for a backcloth for Davenant, *The Siege of Rhodes*. Pen drawing by John Webb. Devonshire Collection, Chatsworth. Reproduced by permission of the Trustees of the Chatsworth Settlement.
43 Painting attributed to John Greenhill, 1663. Collection Ralph Bankes.
44 Engraving by ?William Dolle. Victoria and Albert Museum, London, Enthoven Collection.
46 Painting, seventeenth century. National Portrait Gallery, London.
47 Engraving by Jacobus Houbraken from the first edition of Handel, *Alexander's Feast*, 1738.
48 'Masquerades and Operas.' Engraving by Thomas Cook after William Hogarth, 1807. Raymond Mander and Joe Mitchenson Theatre Collection, London.
49 Contemporary engraving. Victoria and Albert Museum, London, Enthoven Collection.
51 Engraving by Thomas Cook and Son after William Hogarth, 1808. Raymond Mander and Joe Mitchenson Theatre Collection, London.
52 Painting by William Hogarth, *c.* 1731. Tate Gallery, London.
53 Painting by Thomas Frye, eighteenth century. Court House, Warwick.
54 Contemporary engraving. Raymond Mander and Joe Mitchenson Theatre Collection, London.
55 Scene from Feo, ?*Arsace*, Teatro Regio, Turin, 1740. Painting by Pietro Domenico Olivero and collaborators. Museo Civico, Turin.
56 'Disegno del novo Teatro aperto nell'anno 1703 nell'Accademia dell'-Illsmi SS Ardenci.' Etching by Francesco Bibiena from *Varie Opere*, *c.* 1703–8.
57 Contemporary engraving by Matthäus Küsel after Lodovico Burnacini. Victoria and Albert Museum, London, Print Room.
58 Contemporary engraving by Frans Geffels. Raccolta Achille Bertarelli, Milan.
59 Engraving by I. Wagner after L. Amiconi, eighteenth century.
60 Contemporary engraving by Matthäus Küsel after Lodovico Burnacini, Victoria and Albert Museum, London, Print Room.
61 Painting by Pompeo Batoni, *c.* 1762. Collection Murray, Florence.
62 Pen and wash drawing by Fabrizio Galliari. Museo Civico, Turin.
63 Contemporary engraving by Bickart after Giuseppe Galli-Bibiena. Theatermuseum, Munich.
65 From Margaret Baur Heinhold, *Baroque Theatre*, London, 1967.
66 Engraving by Ralph Morghen after Mingardi and Liotard, eighteenth century. Raccolta Achille Bertarelli, Milan.
67 Lithograph by V. Roscioni, nineteenth century. Raccolta Achille Bertarelli, Milan.
68 Painting by Joseph-Sifrède Duplessis, 1775. Collection Comtesse d'Albufera.
69 Painting by Johann Franz Grieppel. Bundesdenkmalamt, Vienna.
70 Drawing by Adolphe Appia, 1926. Schweizerische Theatersammlung, Fondation Adolphe Appia, Berne.
71 Watercolour by Jean-Michel Moreau, 1781. Private collection.
72 Raymond Mander and Joe Mitchenson Theatre Collection, London. Courtesy Institut für Theater Wissenschaft der Universität, Cologne.
73 Painting, *c.* 1580. Drottningholm Museum, Stockholm.
74 Lithograph by V. Roscioni, nineteenth century. Raccolta Achille Bertarelli, Milan.
75 Engraving by J.F. Schröter, eighteenth century. Victoria and Albert Museum, London, Enthoven Collection.
78 Watercolour. Theatermuseum, Munich.
79 Coloured engraving by Carl Postl, 1810. Galerie Liechtenstein, Vienna.
80 Coloured engraving from *Denkmäler des Theaters*, *c.* 1830. Historisches Museum, Vienna.
81 Engraving by Andrea Zucchi, *c.* 1719. Dresden Kupferstichkabinett.
82 Mezzotint after M. Schneider, eighteenth century. Staatsbibliothek, Berlin.
83 Victoria and Albert Museum, London, Enthoven Collection.
84 Drawing by F. Bury, 1800. Nationaler Forschungs- und Gedenkstätten, Weimar.
85 Engraving by 'S.W.', late eighteenth century. Landesbibliothek, Weimar.
86 Lithograph by Alexandre Fragonard, nineteenth century. Victoria and Albert Museum, London. Print Room.
87 Pen and wash drawing by Joseph Platzer, 1786 (facsimile). Victoria and Albert Museum, London, Library. Courtesy Henry Regnery.
88 Aloysia Lange as Zémire in Grétry, *Zémire et Azor*. Contemporary painting by Johann Baptiste Ritter von Lampi the Elder. Private collection.
89 Unfinished painting by Joseph Lange, *c.* 1790. Mozarteum, Salzburg.
90 Engraving by Pietro Bettelini, 1788.
92 Engraving after Winterhalter, nineteenth century.
94 Mary Paton as Susanna in Mozart, *The Marriage of Figaro*, Haymarket Theatre, London, 1822. Contemporary engraving by John Stewart, Victoria and Albert Museum, London, Enthoven Collection.
96 Original MS, completed January 1790. Staatsbibliothek Berlin, Musikabteilung.
98 Engraving by M. Pekenino after N. Roger, nineteenth century.
99 Watercolour, 1781. Theatermuseum, Munich.
100 Pen and wash drawing by Giovanni Bibiena, 1755. Royal Institute of British Architects, Prints and Drawings Department.
102 Pen and wash drawing by Giuseppe Quaglio. Theatermuseum, Munich.
103 Coloured engraving by Joseph Schaffer, 1795.
105 Contemporary coloured engraving by Dutertre after Moreau le Jeune. Bibliothèque et Musée de l'Opéra, Paris.
106 Contemporary engraving by Berthault after Prieur. Raymond Mander and Joe Mitchenson Theatre Collection, London.
107 Pen and watercolour by Giuseppe Quaglio. Theatermuseum, Munich.
109 Watercolour by J. Comelli. Victoria and Albert Museum, London, Print Room.

110 Pen and watercolour, *c.* 1809. Bibliothèque et Musée de l'Opéra, Paris.
111 Pen and watercolour by Lorenzo Sachetti, 1825.
112 *An Avalanche in the Alps*. Painting by Philip Jacob de Loutherbourg, 1803. Tate Gallery, London.
113 Coloured aquatint by Karl Friedrich Schinkel from *Decorationen*, 1819. Victoria and Albert Museum, London, Library.
114 Contemporary aquatint by Alessandro Sanquirico. Victoria and Albert Museum, London, Print Room.
116 Contemporary engraving. Raymond Mander and Joe Mitchenson Theatre Collection, London.
117 Painting, nineteenth century, Liceo Musicale, Bologna.
119 Painting by Rillosi, 1848. Museo Teatrale alla Scala, Milan.
120 Tempera, *c.* 1825. Museo Teatrale alla Scala, Milan.
121 Engraving by J. Thompson, nineteenth century. Victoria and Albert Museum, London, Enthoven Collection.
122 Engraving, 1816. Victoria and Albert Museum, London, Print Room.
123 Coloured lithograph by Le Valentin, nineteenth century. Raccolta Achille Bertarelli, Milan.
124 Victoria and Albert Museum, London, Enthoven Collection.
125 Aquatint, nineteenth century. Raccolta Achille Bertarelli, Milan.
126 Coloured lithograph by Philippe Benoist, mid-nineteenth century. Victoria and Albert Museum, London, Enthoven Collection.
127 Engraving by Rudolph von Alt, 1869.
128 Poster for the first performance of Beethoven, *Fidelio*, Schauspielhaus, Vienna, 20 November 1805.
129 Painting by Ferdinand Georg Waldmüller, 1823.
130 Contemporary coloured and gilt engraving. Victoria and Albert Museum, London, Print Room.
132 Pauline Viardot Garcia as Azucena in Verdi, *Il Trovatore*, Covent Garden, London, 1855. Lithograph. Victoria and Albert Museum, London, Enthoven Collection.
133 Royal Opera House Archives, London.
135 Contemporary engraving. Victoria and Albert Museum, London, Enthoven Collection.
136 Painting, nineteenth century. Museo Teatrale all Scala, Milan.
137 Engraving by Paolo Caselli, nineteenth century. Raccolta Achille Bertarelli, Milan.
138 Watercolour by Carlo Ferario, *c.* 1867.
139 *The Sicilian Vespers*. Painting by Francesco Hayez, 1845. Galleria Nazionale d'Arte Moderna e Arte Contemporanea, Rome.
140 Raccolta Achille Bertarelli, Milan.
141 Cover of the score of Verdi, *Aida*, based on a design by Gerolamo Magnani for the first performance at La Scala, Milan, 1872. Lithograph. Museo Teatrale alla Scala, Milan.
143 Raymond Mander and Joe Mitchenson Theatre Collection, London.
144 Royal Opera House Archives, London.
145 Gouache by the Grieve family, nineteenth century. Victoria and Albert Museum, London, Print Room.
146 Coloured lithograph by Pierre-Luc-Charles Ciceri, *c.* 1831. Bibliothèque et Musée de l'Opéra, Paris.
148 Royal Opera House Archives, London.
149 Photograph from *Le Théâtre*, April 1898. Victoria and Albert Museum, London, Enthoven Collection.
152 Coloured photograph from *Le Théâtre*, July 1898. Victoria and Albert Museum, London, Enthoven Collection.
153 Bust by Jean-Baptiste Carpeaux, nineteenth century. Louvre, Paris.
155 Thames and Hudson Archives.
156 Engraving after Beritze, nineteenth century.
157 Engraving, nineteenth century.
159 Painting by Carl von Piloty, 1865. Bayerische Staatsgemäldesammlungen, Munich.
160 Engraving, 1876.
161 Photograph from *Le Théâtre*, August 1899. Victoria and Albert Museum, London, Enthoven Collection.
162 Watercolour by Max Brückner. Archiv der Richard Wagner Gedenkstätte, Bayreuth.
165 Contemporary engraving.
166 Royal Opera House Archives, London.
167 Photograph from *Le Théâtre*, February 1902. Victoria and Albert Museum, London, Enthoven Collection.
171 Poster for Meyerbeer, *Les Huguenots*, Covent Garden, London, 15 May 1858. Victoria and Albert Museum, London, Enthoven Collection.
175 Scene from *La Reine Christine*, Gripsholm Castle, Sweden, 1785. Watercolour by Louis-Jean Desprez. Bibliothèque et Musée de l'Opéra, Paris.
176–8 Society for Cultural Relations with the USSR, London.
179 Central State Theatrical Museum, USSR.
180 Cover designed by Ivan Bilibin for the score of Rimsky-Korsakov, *The Golden Cockerel*, 1907. Society for Cultural Relations with the USSR, London.
181 Collection Mlle Evelyn Cournand.
183 Engraving from *The Builder*, 7 August 1880. Victoria and Albert Museum, London, Print Room.
185 Photograph in a programme of the Ballets Russes, Champs Elysées Theatre, Paris, 1913. Victoria and Albert Museum, London, Enthoven Collection.
186 Bibliothèque et Musée de l'Opéra, Paris.
187 Reproduced by courtesy of Baron Milo von Watzdorf.
189–91 Society for Cultural Relations with the USSR, London.
198 Goldsmiths' College, London, Library.
199 Raymond Mander and Joe Mitchenson Theatre Collection.
202 Bibliothèque et Musée de l'Opéra, Paris.
203, 204 Society for Cultural Relations with the USSR, London.
205–7 Raymond Mander and Joe Mitchenson Theatre Collection, London.
209 Courtesy Mrs Grygierczyk.
210 Bibliothèque et Musée de l'Opéra, Paris.
212 Raymond Mander and Joe Mitchenson Theatre Collection, London.
213 Photograph from *The Illustrated Sporting and Dramatic News*, 18 April 1931. Raymond Mander and Joe Mitchenson Theatre Collection, London.
214 Raymond Mander and Joe Mitchenson Theatre Collection, London.
215 Photograph from *Le Théâtre*, December 1898. Victoria and Albert Museum, London, Enthoven Collection.
221 Royal Opera House Archives, London.
223, 224 Photographs from *Le Théâtre*, June 1902. Victoria and Albert Museum, London, Enthoven Collection.
229 Raymond Mander and Joe Mitchenson Theatre Collection.
231 Courtesy Mrs Tut Schlemmer.
232 Courtesy Dr Clare Jürgens.
234 Photograph from *Le Théâtre*, July 1898. Victoria and Albert Museum, London, Enthoven Collection.
236 Raymond Mander and Joe Mitchenson Theatre Collection, London.
238 Royal Opera House Archives, London.
240 Courtesy Dr Alessandro Prampolini.
241 Courtesy Erté.
243 Society for Cultural Relations with the USSR, London.

# Photographic Acknowledgments

Architects' Collaborative Inc., Chicago 3. Australian News and Information Bureau, London 252. Austrian National Tourist Office, London 250. Baron Photo Centre Ltd 238. Festspiele Bildarchiv, Bayreuth 156, 157, 165, 168, 253. Rudolf Betz 231. John Blomfield, Bridget d'Oyly Carte Ltd 216. British Broadcasting Co. 239. British Tourist Authority 170. Teatro Colón, Buenos Aires 192. Bulloz 154. Mme J. Colomb-Gérard 36, 37. Courtauld Institute of Art, London 53, 56. Anthony Crickmay 50. Harry Croner 118. Deutsche Fotothek, Dresden 81. Atelier Dietrich 93. Dominic 45, 108, 164, 245. Ellinger 91. Soprintendenza alle Gallerie, Florence 9. Françoise Foliot 181. Freemans 59. Giraudon 25, 27, 34, 35, 68, 153. Guy Gravett, Glyndebourne Festival Opera 17, 101, 104, 220, 228. Louis Held 85. Houston Rogers 246, 247. Ken Howard, Opera Theatre of St. Louis 95. Istituto Italiano di Cultura, London 251. S.F. James, Royal Studios 43. Heinz Köstler, Deutsche Oper, Berlin 233. Lauros-Giraudon 117. Library of the Performing Arts, New York 196, 201, 217. Mansell-Alinari 5, 61. Marconi Co. Ltd 249. Mas 173, 174. Metropolitan Opera Archives, New York 142, 150, 197, 235, 237. Novosti Press Agency 182, 184, 188. Ente Provinciale per il Torismo, Parma 131. Pic 22, 23, 32, 105, 110, 146, 175, 186, 202, 210. E. Piccagliani 76, 77, 115, 134. Universal Editions, Vienna 230. Popperfoto 222. Hertha Ramme 226. Wilhelm Rauh, Festspielleitung Bayreuth 163. Gabinetto Fotografico Nazionale, Rome 135. Soprintendenza alle Gallerie, Rome 139. H.C. Robbins Landon 129. Enar Merkel Rydberg, Kungliga Teatern, Stockholm 249. Salzburger Festspiele Pressbüro 97. Fotoatelier Susan Schimert-Ramme 16. Scottish Opera 147. Nancy Sorensen, Lyric Opera, Chicago 151, Sotheby and Co. 187. Donald Southern 208, 218, 242. *The Times* 239. Foto Studio Sabine Toepffer 225. Eileen Tweedy 10, 21, 30, 39, 49, 57, 60, 75, 83, 86, 87, 94, 109, 112, 124, 126, 130, 132, 136, 145, 149, 152, 161, 167, 171, 183, 185, 215, 223, 224, 234. United States Information Service 194, 195. Musées Nationaux, Versailles 26. Victoria and Albert Museum, London 70. Bildarchiv der Österreichisches Nationalbibliothek, Vienna 90, 92, 98, 103, 111, 127, 128, 158, 169, 211, 219. Opera Society, Washington 193. Archiwum Wydawnictw Teatru Wielkiego, Warsaw 227. John Webb 112, 113, 114, 200, 204. Weltbild 64.

# Index

*Page numbers in italics refer to illustrations*